you are not alone

A Heartfelt
Guide for Grief,
Healing, and Hope

by Debbie Augenthaler

Cover and Book Design by Limor Farber Design Studio

Some names and identifying details have been changed to
protect the privacy of individuals.

Poetry used with permission:
Ellen Bass, "If You Knew" from The Human Line. Copyright © 2007 by Ellen Bass. Reprinted with the permission of The Permissions Company, Inc. on behalf of Copper Canyon Press, www.coppercanyonpress.org.

"For Grief" from TO BLESS THE SPACE BETWEEN US: A BOOK OF BLESSINGS by John O'Donohue, copyright © 2008 by John O'Donohue. Used by permission of Doubleday, an imprint of the Knopf Doubleday Publishing Group, a division of Penguin Random House LLC. All rights reserved.

Ellen Bass, "The Thing Is" from Mules of Love.
Copyright © 2002 by Ellen Bass. Reprinted with the permission of The Permissions Company, Inc., on behalf of BOA Editions Ltd., www.boaeditions.org

"Heavy" from Thirst by Mary Oliver, published by Beacon Press, Boston
Copyright ©2004 by Mary Oliver, used herewith by permission of the
Charlotte Sheedy Literary Agency, Inc.

Excerpted from Out of Solitude by Henri J. M. Nouwen.
Copyright ©1974, 2004 by Ave Maria Press®, Inc., P.O. Box 428, Notre Dame, IN 46556.
www.avemariapress.com. Used with permission of the publisher.

Library of Congress Control Number: 2018940069
ISBN: 978-1-7320233-0-7

www.debbieaugenthaler.com

EVERYSTEP
PUBLISHING

To Jim

Acknowledgments

It's nighttime, and I'm running late for a trip. Rushing outside, I pause for a moment to look up at the dark sky sparkling with stars. In front of me, a black limousine is waiting at the curb. The open door beckons me to slide in on the soft leather seats. Sitting opposite from me are a French couple I've met only once. With no words spoken, I realize I am on my way to France and will be staying at their chateau.

My suitcase doesn't have clothes in it suitable for France, and I don't want to go to a chateau. I'm not a chateau kind of person. I don't know Claudia and Michael well enough to travel with them and their lifestyle is not familiar to me. I begin to panic, digging into my bag for my wallet, which is missing. Just as I realize I need to call home, a phone appears on the leather armrest of door, inviting me to pick it up.

The phone is the old-style phone, heavy and black with a long, curly cord, and when I pick it up and place it to my ear, Jim's familiar and reassuring voice comes out of the receiver.

Hi, honey, he says.

"Jim," I say, "I'm going on this trip and I don't have the right clothes. I don't have my wallet. I'm not prepared for this." My anxiety escalates as I whisper the words, feeling flustered and embarrassed.

"Deb, sweetheart, relax. It's okay." I feel the tension ease away as he reassures me. "You have everything you need—it's all inside of you. And if you find you need something, I promise—I will get it for you."

It's only when I wake up that I remember he is dead.

***

I had this dream in mid-October of 2015, a few weeks before I was going to Kauai, Hawaii, with the intention of writing this book. The impetus to tell this story came from my brother, Dave, who has been living with a terminal illness for the past three years. When he was first diagnosed and doctors told him he had six months to live, Dave told me, "I'm not going to die, but I'm going to live like I'm dying." And he has lived that way ever since.

I immediately made plans to leave behind my private practice and the patients I loved, New York City, family, and friends, to go to Kauai, an ancient island in the middle of the Pacific Ocean. This was the first bold move of many that would follow to live like I was dying. Kauai gave me many gifts, but the number one gift it gave me was time. Time to take a pause, to breathe, and to just be. And time to write the book I've wanted to write since Jim died. Now I was giving myself the space to do it.

Kauai is a beautiful, mystical and sacred island a friend suggested I visit. I'd never been, and I knew no one. I didn't know how to prepare for what was to come. But as Jim promised, everything I needed awaited. I was met with open arms by Kauai. The synchronous events vital to the development of this book and its message of hope began, and continue to this day. To my readers, this book is for you and all your dreams. Dreams do come true.

***

Within my first two weeks of arriving in Kauai, I walked into the living room of Laura Lentz, where she held weekly writing classes (and now online all over the world). The random way we met is one of those synchronistic events that change your life. Through Laura, I met many wonderfully big-hearted people, just like her. Some of them are now part of the team that helped birth this book and all that will follow.

With great gratitude and joy I thank my incredible team of angels. I am humbled by the belief all of you have in me, my book, and the message of hope. My deepest thanks for taking this journey with me. I can't imagine walking this path without any one of you.

Laura, my marvelous mentor, writing teacher, editor, and dear friend—your wholehearted listening and encouragement from the very beginning gave me the courage and confidence to go deep. This book would not be what it is without you. Thank you for all you've done and continue to do to help make my dreams a reality.

April Eberhardt, a true believer and friend the moment we met. Thank you for your tireless navigation in bringing this project to publication and beyond.

Limor Farber, you make words come alive with

your beautiful artistry and design. I'm so glad you were in the living room that night.

Katherine Eid, your devotion, creativity, and talent to our mission and its message is an amazing gift. It's no accident we met. (And another thank you to Laura.)

Manda Pepper Langlinais, how lucky I am that a talented writer like you is also simply the best copy editor ever.

Dearest Shelley. Your love, support, and wisdom throughout my adult life means more than I can ever say. I wouldn't be the me I am today without you. Thank you for holding the space for me all these many years and helping me to discover the courage to pursue my dreams.

To Dr. Jan Seward, thank you for walking by my side on this journey with so much love. To all of my wonderful friends, relatives, soul sisters, and readers who helped shepherd this book to publication: Jennee Miles, Dr. Shelley Reciniello, Laura Gonsalves, Sarah-Valin Bloom, Katrina Anderson, Elizabeth Becker, Ted Box, members of Laura Lentz's Words In Progress Groups: Genoa Bliven, Dainna Cicotello, Alison Downey, Duncan Forgery, Diana Leone, Allen Miller, Lucita Shalev, Larry Tadlock, and the authors of La Poterie Writers Retreat:

Kristen Harnisch, Deborah Burand, Diane Dewey, Eleanor Duffy, Teri Dunphy, and Manda Pepper. (Interestingly enough, in June, 2017, I was invited to this writer's retreat at a chateau in France. This is where the final revisions of the book took shape.)

To my amazing clients—it has been my true honor to work with all of you and gained your trust. Thank you for showing me what true courage and resilience is—and that with hope, everything is possible.

I know how blessed I am that there are more people to thank than there is room for in this space. A special thanks to DearJames®, for instilling in me the belief this book was meant to be; to the wonderful community of people in Kauai who welcomed me with the awesome spirit of aloha while the seeds were blooming; to Jennee Miles, for loving me forever and holding me in the darkest times, to my family and Tulsa angels, to Jim's family, to my dearest friends—you know who you are.

To my brother Dave—your courage and grace continues to inspire me. Thank you for the words that compelled me to understand that now was the time. I love you.

And Jim. Always and forever.

Table of Contents

EMERGING AND TRANSITION

EXPANDING INTO THE MYSTERY

Introduction

This is the book I wish I'd had after my husband Jim died unexpectedly, in my arms, when I was thirty-six and he was only forty-five. He had been healthy and vibrant—the doctors compared the probability of his death from an aortic aneurysm to being struck by lightning. That lightning strike ended my life as I knew it and began the "baptism by fire" that brought me to my new future.

When Jim died, I was shattered. Yet I continued to work and carry on my professional and personal obligations. As a partner at a financial company and stepmother to Jim's two small children, I felt as though I was going through the motions of a life that was now foreign to me without Jim by my side. With the constant love and support of family, friends, and my therapist, I survived this devastating loss, though in the beginning I felt like I would not.

Over time, other people who suffered the loss of loved ones turned to me, seeking solace and wanting to know how to survive the pain. My cousin lost her 14-year-old daughter to cancer. My best friend's husband died of leukemia. And on September 11, 2001, I lost many friends and colleagues. For months following that terrible tragedy, I spent every weekend at funerals and memorial services. Many told me how much I helped them during this time by being present, holding their hands, and empathizing with the devastation they felt. I discovered I could offer comfort to those who are in the midst of pain and grief. All of this led me to change careers and become a psychotherapist specializing in trauma, grief, and loss.

My story of loss is different from your story, yet there are common threads of grief that connect us all. Grief is a natural response to the loss of something or someone. Many of the experiences and feelings from my personal story are similar to the ones I've heard repeatedly from my clients and many others who are grieving. I am sharing my story because I know it will help you to know: you are not alone. When you're grieving, it helps to hear people's stories and how they coped and survived.

Many of you have heard of the stages of grief:

denial, anger, bargaining, depression, and acceptance. But grief is not a linear passage from stage to stage. While these stages are helpful terms to describe reactions we may experience, grief doesn't follow a progression. Grief does not come with a timetable or a rulebook. Friends and family who are worried about you might think you're grieving too much, or too long, or not enough because they cannot see inside your pain or inner turmoil. It's important to know there is no right way or wrong way; however you grieve is the right way for you.

Grief is chaotic and messy and hard. The phases of grief are common denominators in the shared experience of grief. At times you may feel like you're in all the phases at once, bouncing from one phase to another in a minute, an hour, or a day. You may feel like you're progressing and feeling better, and then one small event or memory can tear the thin membrane growing over the wound in your heart and you feel like you're back at the beginning.

And in the beginning many of us are inconsolable. We're distraught and nothing can comfort us. When someone we love dies, it makes no sense—they were there and now they are not. We feel overwhelmed, frightened, and unable to cope, much less be comforted.

Especially in the early phases of grief, we don't believe we'll ever feel better. We can become childlike in our grief, and it takes time to learn how to cope, to heal, and to hope again. Coping with grief is something that has to be learned and developed; if you've never experienced a shattering loss, you have no mental imprint for how to put the pieces back together.

This is a book that speaks to the feelings of grief and offers you tools to cope with inconsolable loss. I will take you into the deep waters of grief and then offer a lifeline to bring you back to shore, to pause and catch your breath. I share my story because when I was newly grieving and traumatized, I wanted to know someone could understand what I was feeling. I couldn't find a book to speak to the part of me that needed to know someone else had felt this way and had survived. I didn't want to read clinical books or books that told me how I should be feeling or what I should be doing. I wanted a book that could witness and validate my experience. Before Jim died, I experienced a lot of loss in my life, but nothing prepared me for losing him. The loss was immeasurable. I wanted someone who "got" what was happening to me. I want you to know: *I get it.*

It took me years to grow from my own losses, and now, coupled with my professional experience and training, I offer healing insights to help guide you through the labyrinth of loss and healing, along with simple suggestions of things to do that can be helpful along the way. I also show how spiritual and metaphysical connections can be forged by loss, revealing the reality that love and spirit never dies.

The distance I have from my grief now gives me a perspective I couldn't have had when I was newly grieving. If you are feeling hopeless in your grief, I want you to pick up this book and know that I have been where you are; I got through it. I made it, and you will make it too.

There are many gifts that come with loss, including spiritual awakenings and discovering the connected bond of eternal love. We often develop a deeper compassion and an appreciation for the blessings that come from the challenging journey of grief, leading us to healing, transformation, and a new kind of joy.

I have walked this path throughout my life and want to walk with you on yours.

Grief is the price we pay for love.

— *Queen Elizabeth II*

Prologue:
The World of Before

Jim was part of my life for almost twelve years. I've never been closer to anyone than I was to Jim. We were great friends before we fell in love. He became my best friend, the person I could tell anything to without fear of judgment. He understood me in ways I almost didn't understand myself. He saw something in me and helped me see it too. He taught me how to trust. To trust in him and to trust in myself. He would tease me, saying, "You're my diamond in the rough."

Jim was so funny, always able to make people laugh. I smile while writing this, thinking of all the laughter we shared and that he shared with others. I always knew when he was on the phone with one of his close friends because he would begin to laugh, and then, unable to stop, he'd lean back in the chair, hand over mouth, or lean over holding his stomach, his eyes wet with amused tears. He was kind, generous, and smart. A wonderful father, brother, son, friend—and husband.

We had loved one another for years but had only been married for two and half of them when he died. I insisted on waiting to marry until I received my undergraduate degree, which I finally did when I was thirty-three. I worked full time and carried a full credit load to finish something I didn't have the opportunity to when I graduated from high school. Jim's huge emotional support during those six years of school and work deepened our relationship. Our love bloomed.

The most exquisitely beautiful moment in my life was on a glorious late spring day in May of 1994. Standing in the vestibule of St. Mary's Church, we could see a carefully chosen circle of close friends and family waiting expectantly. The cantor's beautiful voice filled the church and, with joyful anticipation, I took Jim's hand to begin to step forward. With a gentle tug, he held me back and turned me to face him. With love and tenderness, trembling with emotion, he said, "I want us to have this moment together. This moment just for us. You are making me the happiest man in the world today. I will always love you and cherish you. Thank you for being you and for becoming my wife."

That's the moment we married. The rest was just the icing.

It was very much a mutual relationship, evolving from friendship, to confidantes, to becoming lovers and partners. We each carried wounds from earlier times in our lives. We both needed to learn how to feel safe in love and trust our hearts with each other. I helped save him as he helped save me. When his confidence faltered, I never wavered in believing in him. We supported each other though life's many trials and challenges. Together we knew how.

We knew our union was meant to be.

Debbie Augenthaler

SHATTERED

Whatever grief longing for him brings
Whatever blood Love mixes in his wine
Be grateful; there's one worse fate
Never seeing him once.

— *Rumi (translated by Andrew Harvey)*

~ 1 ~

Those Three Words

"I know we'll be laughing about this tonight," Jim says, reassuring me. He kisses me, caresses my cheek with his hand and holds my gaze. Our eyes lock in silent communion as we hold each other close, in this moment, before the world changes.

Jim looks at me intently, as if he wants to tell me something but cannot find the words. I feel his breath on my cheek as he says, "You know how much I love you."

My heart races up into my throat, pulsing rapidly and making it hard to breathe as a current of unfamiliar energy rushes into the room. "I love you too, so much," I say. "Please let me call an ambulance," I plead again. "Please, Jim."

"No, Deb, I'm really okay," he insists as we embrace and kiss again.

I didn't know this would be our last embrace.

I turn toward the closet to get some clothes, my body attuned with his, when he says, "Debbie, I feel so dizzy."

I spin around to watch him fall backwards onto our bed, right hand on his forehead.

"Stop it, this is not funny, Jim," I say as I jump beside him on the bed. I want to pull this moment into all the other moments Jim plays jokes on me. I want to lighten the dense air pressure that has descended upon our room because Jim is always funny and can make anything better. It would be just like him to try and make me laugh and worry less. He's had a strange sensation in his chest off and on since we woke up. He's not in any pain and thinks maybe it's heartburn and feels foolish going to the hospital. We're only going now because I keep insisting and he won't let me call an ambulance. It's why he thinks we'll be laughing about this tonight. I want him to sit back up and start laughing. I want him to say, "Gotcha!" and then I can be mad at him for scaring me like this.

"Stop it!" I scream, as I straddle him because he hasn't moved. I grab his head with my hands.

A terrible sound comes from his throat, a loud, garbled gargling, and his eyes have rolled back, and I yell, "Look at me, Jim, stop it!" *This cannot be happening.* I reach for the phone on the nightstand. Trembling, I dial 911 and feel the receiver shake against the curve of my ear, hear the fear in my high-pitched voice, and the woman on the other end begins telling me what to do.

"Is the front door open?" she asks.

"No, it's two flights down and I'm not leaving him."

"You must," she insists, "The paramedics need to get in."

"I don't care!" I scream, "They can break the door down, I won't leave him!"

Her voice remains calm and she tells me if I do this they will be able to help him sooner. I drop the phone and race the two flights down and my shaking hand throws open the door. I race back up to Jim and and the telephone three steps at a time.

"Is his tongue in his throat? Pull it back."

Sobbing, I open his mouth and my shaking fingers find his tongue.

"Is he breathing?" she asks.

"I don't know, he's making a noise from his throat,

that's breathing, isn't it? Can't you hear it, isn't that breathing?" A sound I've never heard from a place deep within him.

I press on Jim's chest with both hands as she instructs me in a hard rhythm: press, breathe, press, breathe. Inhaling all of every particle of air in the room. Holy air, breath between life and death. I breathe into his mouth, my lips pressed on his, breathing all of me into him, my whole life force. In between breaths I say fragments of prayers...calling to God and Jesus and Holy Mary, Mother of God, pray for us, begging *please, please, please.*

My arms are filled with the strength of the desperate. I push so hard on his chest. So hard I want him to sit up and say, *Debbie, stop hurting me.*

And finally they arrive. Uniformed men with medical equipment rush into the room, and gentle, firm hands move me aside while they lift Jim from the bed and carefully lower him to the firmness of the floor, between my side of the bed and the door. I push forward to try to see, to be near him, but the paramedics surround him, yelling orders to each other.

"Help him!" I plead as chaos and panic fills the room, bodies moving swiftly, pushing back the unmade bed, their loud voices becoming hushed whispers, police arriving now, officers guiding me to just outside the door, further away from Jim, and asking questions that force me to replay something still in motion. I feel very small and lost in the sea of uniforms and unfamiliar voices.

"When did this happen? Where were you both? Who can we call for you?" Navy blue uniforms with bright metal badges and guns on hips shelter me from the scene just inside the door. With all these people, surely someone can help him.

I insist on going back to Jim. *He needs me.* The paramedics by his side look up with averted eyes, with compassion, their bodies forming a blockade around him, preventing me from getting any closer. I am allowed to kneel on the floor and hold his left foot, as I am desperate to touch him, praying and crying, kissing his exposed foot so he knows it's me. *This cannot be happening.*

Sirens and strangers invading intimate moments. The darkness of early dawn now turning into a soft sunrise blue as I walk outside, looking up at the clear late-October chill. Disoriented, with neighbors all around, "What can we do? What do you need?" Jim now on a gurney and they still won't let me near him. *Why? He needs me, he needs to see me.* "Jim," I shout, "Jim, I'm right here! Everything is going to be fine, we're going to the hospital now!"

My voice rises as my throat closes. I follow to climb in the back of the ambulance with him and they gently hold me back. "I am his wife," I say, "I am going with him." It's increasingly difficult to speak. There is no room in my chest for breath. A paramedic asks a neighbor to drive me. NO. A police officer offers to drive me. *NO.* I scream *I. AM. HIS. WIFE. You will not take him without me!* I ride in the front of the ambulance for the five-minute drive to North Shore Hospital.

Jumping out of the ambulance, I run to the back as they lift Jim out, desperate to see him, to tell him he's going to be okay, to let him know I'm there. Someone holds my arm to keep me back as they open the back doors and run with him on the gurney into the emergency room. I can't see him through the uniforms, and I pull my arm away and run after. A doctor stops me as I try to trail them down the hallway and tells me I must wait for Jim's brother who will be there any minute.

I am not allowed to go where they are taking Jim.

The doctor gently tells me they are doing all they can. This means they are trying to save his life. This means Jim is alive. Jim's brother comes rushing into the

ER, and we hug and cry and are escorted down the hallway and enclosed in a little white box of a room.

They leave us to pray and hope. Waiting to be told he is going to be okay. Soon, too soon, through the small square window in the door, I see doctors in white coats walking down the long hallway towards us. Their downcast faces tell me they will open the door to say something unspeakable. Unthinkable. Unbearable. My heart lurches, flailing wildly in my chest, pounding up into my head, and panic takes over.

Turning away before they can open the door, I try to push through hardness of white sterile wall. Pressing my hands with the force of denial, trying to push my way through solid cement, whimpering no, no, no, his brother praying, *our father who art in heaven hallowed be thy name. Oh my god,* I'm stuck, help me, the primal instinct to flee screaming inside my head to get away, *get me out, get me out, get me out, let me out.*

If I can get out of this room they can't tell me.

The door opens. No. I whimper, clutching my stomach, folding into myself, unable to breathe. I recoil, my back to them, my head pressed against the cold, hard, unforgiving wall, my body deflated with defeat, Jim's brother trying to hold me, keep me here as I feel myself drifting away, diving deeply in my mind to another place where I don't have to hear or see or think. Death is so close I can feel its breath on my neck, so close I can smell my own fear.

I want to freeze time. *Please don't let the next moment come. Go away.*

Inevitably, the softly spoken words fill the tiny room. "He is dead. I'm sorry, we did everything we could." The words, finally out in the open, create a vacuum around me and the world is far, far away.

He is dead. With these three words, I am no longer who I was.

With these three words, my husband, my beloved, my best friend, my future with him, the father of the child we were trying to conceive, is gone. I didn't know until weeks later he died instantly—his soul flying out the window as he fell backwards onto our bed.

When his soul flew out the window part of mine did too.

His mother arrives and they tell her. We hold each other, wordless. They lead us to another windowless, airless room. I push open the door and walk in to see him. Alone. His mother and brother offer me this time with him first.

Alone with his body, now on a bed. A white sheet rests over his chest, covering evidence of all they tried to revive him. Only his bruised throat and head are exposed. His loving deep brown eyes now closed. *He is dead.*

I run my hands along his face, stroking his cheek, his forehead, smoothing his hair. My tears falling on his still face. Maybe my fingers can still draw something from his body to fill up the gaping hole ripping mine apart. My love, oh Jim, how could this be? *He is dead.* I lay my cheek next to his, weeping. In disbelief, in despair, in deep love.

I stroke his arms, his hands, I want to crawl in the bed and curl up against him. I want to, but I don't, because I know he's not there. He is dead, but his body is still warm. Less than an hour ago he promised me we would be laughing together tonight.

I hold his beautiful head in my hands, weeping. I kiss his forehead. I kiss his eyes. Finally, I softly kiss his still tender lips with mine.

This is our last kiss.

Moving Through the Chaos

The moments before and the moments right after someone you love dies are etched in your mind with crystal clarity. If you weren't present when they died, then you will still remember how and when you were told, where and what you were doing. Often our memory becomes cloudy afterwards, when we are grieving and struggling to make sense of a world without the person we love.

When someone you love dies, it's almost impossible to believe, especially if it's sudden and unexpected. The shock is enormous and overwhelming. Anticipated death (of someone who is terminally ill) is also a shock, just in a different way. The last few days, hours, and minutes spent with our loved one takes on great meaning.

Death is difficult to comprehend. We deny, we bargain, we plead, we weep, we ask why, we want to push Death away— all of these "stages" happening in seconds, wrapped in moments.

Looking back, I am now grateful Jim and I had that last moment together, to say I love you one more time. I am grateful that I was with him, to know he didn't suffer, he had no pain, and no fear. He was not alone. I know this is a gift.

for you

I replayed in my mind a million times what I might have done differently, a running loop which added to the pain and helplessness I felt. How could I not save him if I was with him? The what ifs and if onlys. What if I had done this or that? If only he had said yes when I first suggested going to the hospital. He thought it was heartburn. He had no pain while his heart was taking its last beats. The doctors said he would have died even if he had been in the hospital. Moments I relived multiple times a day for months, long after I was told there was nothing I could do.

Do you have a running loop racing through your mind? It's a natural response; because the world feels scary and out of control. We feel helpless and wish we could change the outcome. However, no matter what the circumstances are, the what ifs and if onlys will not change the outcome. The running loop may continue to happen for a while, but it will ease.

Take deep breaths. Be as kind and gentle to yourself as you possibly can. It's what you need right now.

Third Eye Kiss
by Debbie Augenthaler

while i dance with memories
your face your forehead
that spot right there in the center

that last night
i stood behind while you sat in a chair
and leaned down
and kissed that spot
right there in the center
of your face your forehead

my arms coming from behind
wrapping around your shoulders
snug and close
another kind of dance
between us

you leaning back
knowing your smile
even though i couldn't see it
i knew it was there

i know your smile
that one just for me
will always be
even if i can't see it
i know it's there

You are 'there', I 'here'. Worlds separate us,
Death's angels, the void of space...
Yet I say your name, and waves of Light
Wash to me silently from your Heart.

— *Rumi (translated by Andrew Harvey)*

~ 2 ~

The First Night

Dazed, with Jim's gold wedding band now on my left middle finger, I clutch the plastic bag tightly to my chest and climb into the back seat of his brother's car. The harsh glare of the sun stings as we walk out of the hospital. Bright, searing sun. It has moved across the sky since the early morning, yet somehow this surprises me.

I am still reeling from what happened right after those precious moments alone with Jim. The doctors asked if Jim wanted to be an organ donor, because if he did, they needed to act immediately.

"Did Jim have the flu? Has he been sick the past few days? What did you do yesterday?"

I answered questions through sobs, learning he wouldn't be able to donate major organs because he'd been dead for an hour. Yet there was so much else Jim could give, they explained, asking me to sign various documents. It's only minutes after being told he is dead, only minutes after kissing his lips. I can't imagine the eyes of my beloved, his skin, and veins, any part of him, in anyone else's body. *He is my husband.* His skin, his hair, his eyes—I wanted all of him intact so he could come back. *It was all a terrible mistake, wasn't it? How can this be real? He told me an hour ago we'd be laughing tonight.*

I pushed my denial aside to sign the papers so they could begin changing someone else's life, which is what Jim wanted. The generosity of Jim, even in death, always shone through.

And right after that the nurse handed me a small plastic bag and Jim's wedding ring, and my legs gave way. A nurse helped me as I sat down on the cold tiles of the hospital floor. Other nurses rushed over, and I could hear them deciding if they need to admit me, to sedate me, to let me finally escape from reality. His brother and I exchanged a look, and he lifted me up. We needed to go tell Jim's children.

Now, slumped in the back seat, I inspect the contents of the bag: his favorite worn brown leather braided belt, his wallet, his watch. His clothes were cut off during the attempts to revive him and are not in the bag. I arrived at the hospital earlier this morning with my husband on a gurney. I leave now with only a small plastic bag.

I hear loud denials of disbelief from distant voices, "Oh no, no!" as his brother makes painful phone calls, repeating the words, "Jim has died." Anguished cries from the phone amplify within the car. His mother weeps quietly in the front seat.

***

Arriving at our townhouse, I enter a parallel world. How can it look the same when everything has changed? We go upstairs to the kitchen, stunned as shock settles in. We sit in the hollowness, wondering how this can be real, and wait for people to arrive.

The day becomes a buzzing blur of chaos and warmth with family and friends surrounding me, flying and driving in from all over the country, swarming into the hive of my home, bringing food and tears, and holding my grief while I try to hold theirs too.

I need a moment alone. I walk up the second flight of stairs to our bedroom. Halfway up, when my eyes fall even with our bedroom floor, I can see long strips of gauze, ripped paper, and other debris from the medics who tried to save Jim scattered on the floor. I walk to the doorway of the room we shared and see spots of blood scattered on the cream-colored rug beneath our bed.

Turning away, I make it halfway down and sink to the stairs. While I sit and weep, caught between two worlds—my old world with Jim and the new one I cannot face alone—Father Paul, our parish priest, slips by me and quietly cleans the chaos from the room.

When he is finished, I go in alone. It is still. Like standing inside a picture. I stare at the phone on the unmade bed—*push, breathe, push, breathe*—and at the photos of us in Martha's Vineyard, our tanned faces with wide smiles, arms around each other, wind whipping through our hair, the lighthouse in the background. The mirror leaning atop the pine dresser reflects the emptiness of the room. I am standing there but I do not see myself. I see the two of us picking out this mirror in the antique store in Connecticut. I see Jim adjusting his tie in this mirror and combing his neatly cut brown hair.

There is an alarm clock on the nightstand by Jim's side of the bed, announcing the hour and minutes with red numbers. The numbers continue to change, but for me time is frozen in the moment when he fell backwards onto the bed. Frozen in the moments that are captured in the photos, in the mirror. The clock marks something I am no longer a part of.

Push, breathe, push, breathe.

It is dark outside. I ask my Aunt Jennee if she will sleep with me in our bed, on Jim's side. After many years of sleeping and waking together, this is my first night without him. My tears will not, cannot, stop. My body is in high survival mode, heart racing, terror tingling in every cell, the whole of me clenched tight and closed, not wanting to absorb the enormity of what has happened.

Jennee is exhausted from having flown across the country to be with me as she has flown across many lifetimes to protect me, and I her. She loves Jim too, and was by my side at the altar when we spoke our vows: 'til death do us part. She is more than family—she is my mentor, supporter, guardian angel. Jennee shares my pain this first night, and after our eyes are swollen and our throats are hoarse from grief, she falls asleep.

I want to be alone with my thoughts. I stare at the ceiling, willing this to be a terrible mistake. I look at the framed wedding picture on my nightstand, Jim so handsome in his black tuxedo and me in a cream-colored beaded dress, both of us always smiling, always touching. So alive together. I think of our joyful, intimate wedding, with just our closest family and friends invited to celebrate with us. And now we are all gathered together again, two and half years later, in shock and terrible grief.

I desperately want to know he is okay. I begin praying and pleading in silence so I won't wake Jennee. *Please let him come back.* It is all a horrible mistake, isn't it? *God, please, I can't live without him.* All day I have wanted to know how he is, where is he, is he okay?

The clock insists that time has passed—3 a.m., 4 a.m., each number marks an hour into the meaningless vacuum of time. My world has become a time of before and after. That's all there is. I begin to bargain with a God who doesn't seem to be listening. *Please let him come back*, I beg, *please, God.* I squeeze my eyes shut hard because I have become a child in my grief, clenching my fists, my body rigid. Jennee is breathing next to me, and I pray, *please let it be Jim beside me,* as if he will magically reappear.

Opening my eyes, I see Jennee is still there, un-moving aside from her breathing. At that point, I give up on God and start talking directly to Jim.

Jim, I need a sign, please come back, even for a second, I just need to know you are okay. Please. My love, are you okay?

While these words race through my mind, my skin feels the energy shift in the room. I am lying on the sheets, my face pressed into the smell of Jim. Jennee surprises me by rolling toward me, her eyes still closed in sleep, and she puts her left arm over my chest. Like Jim did.

She says, "I love you, Deb." Like Jim did.

I hold my breath as she rolls back to his side of the bed. I whisper into the night air, "Jennee, are you awake?" There is no answer but the soft intake of breath. A familiar breathing.

The red numbers on the clock keep moving, the photographs keep looking back at me in the dark, and eventually the sun rises, and dawn's muted light creeps in again through the window in the bedroom. Just like it had twenty-four hours earlier. It feels like seconds ago. It

23

feels like many lifetimes ago.

I wait for Jennee to wake up. She reaches out to hold me, and I ask if she remembers saying I love you in the dark. She does not.

Straddling Two Worlds

Jim gave me a sign in the moment I needed it most—he loved me from somewhere else and wanted me to know. I only told the few who would understand because I was afraid people would think I was crazy. I already felt like I was going crazy trying to comprehend this new world of After. I was filled with overwhelming pain, grief, and fear.

When you have trouble facing reality and are straddling the two worlds—the Before and the After—you cling to the Before, not ready to move into the After. It is overwhelming to face the reality of what's happened. The liminal space. Often, when in this space, things happen that are magical and mystical. Let small miracles help guide and comfort you as you adjust to a new reality.

Countless people have experienced and found solace in it. Many people talk about being visited by their loved ones. My grandmother always talked about my grandfather visiting her the night after he died. She woke up and he was standing at the foot of her bed to let her know he was okay. No one ever questioned this. There are innumerable stories about visitations, either ones like my grandmother described or powerful visitation dreams. Many people who lost loved ones on 9/11 have spoken or written extensively about this.

My clients who are grieving talk about these kinds of experiences and want to know if it's normal. "Of course it is," I tell them. Now I'm telling you the same.

I encourage my clients, and you, to continue looking for signs as the months and years pass. If you're open to receiving a sign you'll often have one. Spirit lives on. The connected bond of love doesn't end.

There are many ways we can continue to experience this connection. Through dreams, songs, scents, finding something special in odd places. In nature. Whenever I see a white butterfly I know it's my Aunt Judy reminding me of our everlasting connection. Be open to see what comes. You will know.

for you

When we're in crisis, time seems to stop, turning into frozen moments, a cluster wound tightly inside our bodies. These moments are forever frozen with crystal clear clarity. Be aware of their power—they are very easily "triggered" and can cause you to feel like you're re-experiencing a trauma all over again.

For example, even now when I hear sirens and ambulances it takes me right back to that morning, in vivid detail. In the early days it happened often. The triggers would take me by surprise. Just seeing a photo of a wedding or hearing a favorite song of ours was enough to cause me to crumble into sobs. Triggers can bring back all the feelings and emotions instantly and often surprise you with their intensity. The body always remembers. Know this will happen and be gentle with yourself. Know this is normal.

Take deep breaths. If possible, take some private time and let yourself feel the feelings, cry, pound a pillow, whatever feels right to release stored up emotions inside.

Be as kind and gentle to yourself as you possibly can. It's what you need right now.

When you lose someone you love,
Your life becomes strange,
The ground beneath you becomes fragile,
Your thoughts make your eyes unsure;
And some dead echo drags your voice down
Where words have no confidence
Your heart has grown heavy with loss;
And though this loss has wounded others too,
No one knows what has been taken from you
When the silence of absence deepens.

— *John O'Donohue*

~ 3 ~

Widow Falling

In the days following Jim's death, the simple act of standing or walking becomes incredibly challenging, as though my body is being blown down by the howling winds of grief. I am living in two parallel worlds, straddling them—the before life I shared with Jim, and the shocking world of life without him. Each step toward my new life creates another wound, another gash of pain. *Is this really happening? He's dead?*

The wake of loss widens far beyond me. Jim was one man but had played so many roles in so many lives. Jim was my husband, but he was also father, son, brother, nephew, cousin, friend, and colleague. Hundreds of people reach out in sorrow, a shared grief weaving us together.

I collapse four times in those first few days. Jim's brother is there to hold me up, or maybe we hold each other up. The first time my legs fail me is when the doctors walk down the long hallway to give us the news. The second time is right after the nurse hands me the plastic bag just before we leave the hospital.

The third time is the next day when Jim's mother, brother, and I go to the funeral home. I have to make sure everything is just right for Jim—the service, the details, the coffin, the flowers, the suit he will wear, the songs that will be sung. I try to be strong, but feel like I am outside of my body going through the motions. As soon as I do feel myself back inside my body, my legs begin to weaken, as if my infrastructure is gone without him by my side.

Jim's brother and I go downstairs to choose the casket. His mother stays upstairs because choosing the casket for her son is too much for her to bear. Caskets are lined up with overhead lights shining on them—empty caskets waiting for bodies. Stainless steel, dark mahogany trimmed in gold, cherry, oak, pine, each with white and cream soft satin interiors. The funeral director stands behind us as we walk among them, his jarring voice asking us if we see anything we like. *Any I like?* Unfathomable.

I cannot do this. This means it's real, it's not a dream, he's really dead.

That's when my legs collapse, like thin reeds in a hurricane. Jim's brother holds me up, encouraging me to finish this task as I begin to wail.

Through his own tears, he says, "You can do this. We'll do it together."

And then the dreaded viewing, before the wakes begin. Slow steps to reach the casket, with cream satin fabric surrounding him. I know he will be wearing the dark suit his best friend and I had picked out from our closet, the red and navy tie, the crisp white shirt. Each step walking toward the casket is like I am walking closer to the world of After. I cannot look. I must look. I cannot look. Now I'm at the casket and there he is, but it's not Jim. It's his face and suit and mouth and hair and arms and legs. I lean over and reach out to touch him one last time. *My love.* My hand shakes as I touch his cold skin, the face I cherish. His face is masklike and too still with too much makeup.

Yet I smooth the hair along his forehead, run my hand along his chest, fix his tie slightly. I slip his wedding ring, along with a few pictures, into the pocket of his suit jacket because I know he would want to be buried with it.

My chest constricts so painfully I cannot breathe. And that's when my legs fail me again, and this time Jim's brother and I are holding each other up.

At the funeral I manage to walk down the aisle at St. Mary's Church, supported by his brother and mother and the knowledge that I have to be strong for Jim. Hundreds of grieving eyes focus on us with great sorrow. The same aisle Jim and I had joyfully walked together two and a half years earlier at our wedding. Today I am following his casket. The memory of that joy is a pain searing my heart, as I think of our beautiful moment of love before we said our vows.

We had chosen *"One Hand, One Heart"* as our wedding song.

> "Now it begins, now we start
> One hand, one heart;
> Even death won't part us now."

Today the same cantor sings. Her beautiful voice, so gloriously perfect on our wedding day, squeezes sorrow from the songs she sings today: "Ave Maria." "Be Not

Afraid." "Wind Beneath My Wings." Father Paul, who married us, is now presiding over Jim's funeral.

Jim's close knit group of friends, many of them pallbearers, ask if they can wear burgundy and gold fezzes when they carry his casket down the aisle. The fezzes were an essential item worn during the annual trip Jim and his friends would take every year. They called it the fishing trip but it was really an excuse to get together to laugh, play poker, drink, and act like college kids again. It is a perfect tribute from his friends. I know Jim saw it and smiled. A little moment of levity, reminding everyone of Jim's humor, his smile, and his love of laughter. They walk his casket to the front of the altar with strength and devotion holding them up.

So many friends and family surrounding and holding me, and I am grateful. But the one person I want most to be here and hold me is Jim. I want him to comfort me. I want to turn to him as I have turned to him over the years, and yet I can't.

As each day goes by, the impact of my loss grows. Not only is my husband gone, I have lost my best friend, my lover, my rock. I have lost our future together. Now I have to confront the reality alone.

I don't know any 36-year-old widows. How can I be a widow if I still feel married? If I keep hoping beyond reason that Jim is coming back? I don't want to believe that time can keep marching forward, though the red numbers on the clock keep insisting it is so. I am a widow walking in the wilderness—in the void between the world of Before and the world of After.

***

For a couple of days, I hold onto the hope it is possible I can be pregnant. I won't take the sleeping pills offered; I won't drink any wine. If I am carrying Jim's baby, part of him will still always be with me. I've been taking the fertility drug Clomid for seven months, and we'd been making love with the intention of building a family together the weekend before he died. I cradle my belly and pray for our child. I tell the baby how much it is loved, how much we want it. The only hope I have of surviving the world of After.

The crushing blow at the doctor's when he says I am not pregnant is a different kind of grief. I feel a visceral churning deep in my empty womb. To have part of our dream of a family is better than no dream.

Who am I now? I am not a wife anymore. I am not a mother to Jim's child. I am a widow. To prove my new title, here is the death certificate. The typed words on white paper, confirming what my legs, what my body, what my whole soul is learning, every day. Pronounced dead: Oct. 28th, 1996. Hour: 6:50AM. Immediate cause: Acute cardiac failure. Surviving Spouse: (if wife, provide maiden name). How cruel it is to see my maiden name typed in, as if my legal name, my married name, no longer matters.

In the weeks ahead I check the box for widow on all the paperwork that comes with death. At the bank and at the lawyer's office, and other places I can't remember now. Over and over and over.

Jim is gone and with him went our dreams of the kind of life we would build together.

Who Am I Now?

You will discover more losses along the way to healing. It will feel like a fresh new wound, for each loss merits its own mourning. Especially when you lose your partner, your self-identity changes. To ask, "Who am I now?" is to begin facing all the other losses you will encounter.

This inundation of loss can feel like a flood that overwhelms us. This is natural and understandable. When our anxiety escalates in this way, our brain is wired to interpret it as danger and our bodies respond by going into survival mode. This causes the "thinking" part of our brain (the prefrontal cortex) to shut down, and we can only feel, unable to think clearly. This often causes anxiety or panic attacks, including the feeling of not being able to breathe.

It's important each loss is recognized and mourned. There's no right way or wrong way; often it's just knowing that, "Yes, feeling like I don't know who I am anymore is all a natural part of this."

Though I was officially a widow, I still felt married to Jim. I wore my wedding and engagement rings for a long time. I don't remember exactly when I decided it was time to stop. What I do remember is how difficult it was to stop wearing the rings. I remember the day I took them off. And then put them back on the next day. Alternating for a while until I knew it was time to leave them off for good. Another painful goodbye. Eventually I had the stone from my engagement ring made into a necklace so I could wear it every day, closer to my heart. I wear it still.

for you

Take a deep breath. Whenever you feel like you can't breathe, stop what you are doing and inhale deeply, as deeply as you can. Exhale. And then take another deep breath. Continue doing so until you feel you can breathe more easily.

Give yourself time. Be compassionate and kind to yourself. And let people help you. Let them help bolster and support you. Whether it is a family member, a friend, or a professional, it's immensely helpful to have someone to lean on, who will listen with love and support.

When you're ready, grieve each loss in your own way, one that feels right for you.

Be as kind and gentle to yourself as you possibly can. It's what you need right now.

Debbie Augenthaler

GRIEVING and COPING

The answers quick and keen, the honest look,
the laughter, the love,—
They are gone. They are gone to feed the roses.
Elegant and curled
Is the blossom. Fragrant is the blossom.
I know. But I do not approve.
More precious was the light in your eyes than
all the roses in the world.

— *Edna St. Vincent Millay*

~ 4 ~

Please Come Back

Jim, please come back. I can't move without you.

It is late afternoon on the day after he died. We have returned from the funeral home, and now I am in our bed, sapped of strength, feeling paralyzed from shock. Not yet knowing just how much strength I will need for the wakes and the funeral. From downstairs, I hear the soft voices of my angels, the hum of their words creating an invisible foundation of loving support. Their energy underneath me holds me. After the sirens, the shouting, the sound of my own voice screaming, I want quiet, but chaos echoes in the loop of what ifs and if onlys racing through my mind.

I crave silence. I've come to my room to mute the

ringing phones, doorbells, clanging dishes being stacked, clinking glasses, pots and pans being sorted out. Angels making preparations for all the people who will be coming the next few days. These are the new sounds of grief—friends and family gathered downstairs. It's too much for me. The smell of food winding its way up the stairs makes me nauseous.

I need soft, and soft comes into my room in the soothing voice of Jennee coming to check on me. I open my eyes to look into hers when I feel the gentle strokes of her hand on my hair, her soothing words in my ear. "I'm here for you, just rest." I begin shaking again, awakening to the reality that I have just returned from the funeral home after picking out his casket, after choosing the clothes Jim will wear inside of it. She responds to my thoughts, because I cannot speak, cannot form the words that touch her ears without sound: *please hold me, soothe me, keep me here, I must make sure everything is taken care of for him.*

Jim, please come back.

It is difficult to engage with anyone, like being really high or heavily medicated, although I have yet to take a pill or sip any alcohol. I am numb from grief, and trying to comprehend the last twenty-four hours completely overwhelms me. The weight of grief is settling into my body and right now it's hard to sit up. It hurts to breathe. So I lay here, in our bedroom. The room we shared, the room we no longer share. In one swift second, he died.

I couldn't save you, Jim.

I feel separate from everyone, no matter how strong their love. Even Jennee. It's as if I am in a place very far away, drowning in my own pain. Where have I gone? I am different now, in an instant becoming someone I don't recognize. The rest of the world feels divided from me by an invisible force field. I want to stay in the world of Before and not be in the world of After, but I'm some place in between—alone, in a foggy haze. Part of me wants to fly out the window and follow Jim. I feel like part of me has.

Jim, I'm taking care of everything for you. I know you still need me here.

As soon as my soul cried out for them, my angel tribe came. And I know they won't leave until I ask them to. They hold me in love, in sorrow, in grief, their angel wings enfolding me. They are the gravity holding me on earth when I want to float away and be anywhere but here.

I cannot bear this, Jim. But for you, I will.

My angel friends, all of us close in age, met when we were very young, at our first professional jobs. We never thought something like this would happen to one of us. We were happy for one another, falling in love, marrying and sharing the next phases of life. Some of us with children, one newly pregnant and unable to share her joy that week, knowing Jim and I had been trying to have our own child.

They are grieving with me, they are heartbroken too, and instinctively know what I need. They take care of everything—thanking the many people with generous offers of help on my behalf, answering the phone that doesn't stop ringing, running errands, and opening their homes to out-of-town friends. Planning four wakes, a funeral, and a reception for hundreds of people. Their stricken, pale faces, worry lines deepening with every detail, their own wings wilting. They hold each other up and me.

I was in a cocoon of protection, and they filtered contact with the outside world to keep me insulated from anything not absolutely necessary.

Jim, please come back. I am so scared.

Each time I wake up, I have a second or two of relief before connecting with the slap of memory—*he's dead, I couldn't save him.* The memory reel plays over and over and over, and they listen as angels do, as if hearing it for the first time.

Jim, I'm sorry I couldn't save you.

The fog lifts for moments, long enough for us to select photographs for the wakes and funeral—pictures of him as a child, a teenager with long hair, photos of him with his mother and brother and sisters and their newborn children, of us on our wedding day—the arc of his life in my hands. The fog lifts long enough to bring up funny stories—how Jim would make a funny monster face and chase the kids, who ran laughing through their screams, all around the house on holidays. We laugh, we cry, and then we laugh again.

Jim loved to laugh and would have wanted to see us laughing, even now. After the funeral, we gather in the kitchen for one last night together, consuming copious amount of wine. Telling more stories. The story of the burgundy fezzes worn by the pallbearers, work stories, tequila shot stories, dancing stories... It becomes a rhythm of grief—story, laughter, wine, tears; story, laughter, wine, tears.

Early the next morning, everyone is sleeping off the alcohol and sorrow. I make my way into the kitchen and pick up a glass to wash it. As soon as I do, it strikes me how senseless and absurd the act of washing this glass is. What is the use of cleaning dishes, of any kind of order? *Jim is gone, he's dead.* I put the glass back into the sink and stare at it. The glass represents something I cannot express with words. I look out the window and see the red and brown leaves, once green, getting ready to drop from the branches, and I slide down to the floor, weeping.

Oh, Jim, my heart, please come back.

People begin leaving. It is a crisp, clear, cloudless blue autumn sky. So like the day he died. My angel tribe is concerned about leaving me alone, insisting someone needs to stay with me, but I want to be alone. I need to be alone with my grief. All week I've had to hold back my own sounds of deep grieving and I've held back the wails. I have cried more in six days than my entire life, but now I need the freedom to wail.

At the four wakes, standing with his family for hours, we greet hundreds of people who come to pay their respects. I keep it together with silent tears, accepting the hugs, the pressed palms, saying thank you for the words of sympathy. At his funeral, I try to be strong and don't make a scene, wearing a classic black dress covering up a body melting with grief, the messiness of grief. I crave time alone, to be messy, to be weak, to wail, to keen. To not subdue myself, to mourn uninterrupted.

When I am finally alone, the house is stark and empty. All the flowers are removed at my request, as I am sickened by the scent of the lilies. So quiet. So alone. So empty. I slowly walk upstairs. I open our closet to look at his clothes and run my finger along his empty sleeves. His shoes are in a neat row. I hug his suit jackets and pull them into my body, feeling the texture on my cheek. I go to his pine chest and pull out all the drawers. My hand floats over the softness of his neatly folded tee shirts and socks and underwear. Everything is the same as it was a week ago.

Except he is gone.

It finally comes, from deep within my soul, a visceral force coming from the depth of a place none of us ever want to visit, but most of us will some day. The death wail, the keening. My mouth opens like a volcano and I scream. I pull out the shirt he'd worn last from the laundry hamper and hold it up to my face. I let this force overtake my whole shaking body.

Jim, Jim, Jim.

I wear his shirt until it doesn't smell like him anymore.

Suspended In The Fog

I am grateful for the outpouring of love and support I had. My angel tribe, friends and family, did all they could do help me through the most difficult time of my life. Let people help you. Let them do all you can't.

When we experience any kind of traumatic loss it feels like we are in an alternate reality. It's hard to think clearly or concentrate—our bodies are in survival mode and the thinking part of our brain (the prefrontal cortex) "shuts down." Our nervous system is hyper-aroused; we experience anxiety or panic attacks, can feel our hearts pounding, and the running loop races round and round in our minds as we try to integrate what has happened. Eventually exhaustion takes over and we "crash." It's difficult to speak, to "see" through the fog induced by psychological shock.

We're still in disbelief, unable to accept reality. The

world feels scary and out of control. Many of us feel like we are in a place of in-between, pleading and praying this isn't true, that when we wake up it will all be as it was before. It takes time to accept this new reality, so we are suspended in limbo. Everything has changed and it's almost impossible to connect with a world that keeps continuing. I prayed for Jim to come back, even after the funeral, knowing he was dead. The magical thinking persists—just because days have passed does not mean you're ready to accept the reality.

In our modern society, there is an expectation of trying to keep it together—be stoic, have a stiff upper lip, try to be strong. At Jim's funeral, I was stoic, adhering to what I call the unwritten rules of grief: please don't make a scene, don't make us uncomfortable, please keep the messiness private. These rules are to help others feel more comfortable with YOUR grief. But grief IS messy. We want to wail and keen. And it's healthy to do so, to let it out and to feel your feelings.

Many cultures acknowledge this basic human need when grieving. Some cultures call it the death wail. Others, keening. Wailing and keening. It's a traditional part of public mourning in many societies, a vocal lament for the dead. And don't we all want to wail, want to scream out in agony and sorrow over the loss of someone dear to us?

I shared my despair with a relative the morning after he'd died. "What's the point of anything? I don't want to live in a world without Jim." This was a reasonable, natural feeling after he'd died in my arms. But she became very concerned, thinking I wanted to kill myself. That wasn't what I meant; I was sharing how despondent I felt, a normal reaction to the death of my husband, my life partner. It's how I felt in the moment—it's natural to have thoughts like this. Imagining the world without the person you love is beyond comprehension in the first few days.

A wail would have expressed the same pain, just without words.

for you

Let people help you as much as possible. It's okay to not be okay.

Make a list of things that need doing that you can't put off. And if you're not ready to do any of them, ask someone to do it. Have the list ready because sometimes, when someone asks, your mind goes blank and you don't remember. When we're grieving, it's hard to focus and it's hard to concentrate. You may find yourself walking into a room and completely forget why. This happened to me often. Grieving is hard, it's exhausting, it takes all of your energy.

Honor what your body is telling you. I wanted to be involved in all the planning because I wanted everything to be "just right" for Jim. I know that being involved in the details gave me the tiniest sense of having some kind of control over something. Because the world felt completely out of control. I could at least have a say in how we honored and celebrated his life. But not everyone is capable of doing so. If you don't feel able to do this and have people who can handle the arrangements for you that's fine too. Whatever feels right for you!

Give yourself the space and time to keen and wail. Feel your feelings. It's what you need right now.

If You Knew
by Ellen Bass

What if you knew you'd be the last
to touch someone?
If you were taking tickets, for example,
at the theater, tearing them,
giving back the ragged stubs,
you might take care to touch that palm,
brush your fingertips
along the life line's crease.

When a man pulls his wheeled suitcase
too slowly through the airport, when
the car in front of me doesn't signal,
when the clerk at the pharmacy
won't say Thank you, I don't remember
they're going to die.
A friend told me she'd been with her aunt.
They'd just had lunch and the waiter,
a young gay man with plum black eyes,
joked as he served the coffee, kissed
her aunt's powdered cheek when they left.

Then they walked half a block and her aunt
dropped dead on the sidewalk.

How close does the dragon's spume
have to come? How wide does the crack
in heaven have to split?
What would people look like
if we could see them as they are,
soaked in honey, stung and swollen,
reckless, pinned against time?

What I long for, you know would kill me;
What I think will kill me, you know will heal me.
Loving you, I enter a darkness where I can't see anything.
"You do not need to; I am guiding you by the hand."

— *Rumi (translated by Andrew Harvey)*

~ 5 ~

Cinnamon Toast

My body shuts down the moment Jim dies.

Someone hands me a glass of water and I don't think I can swallow it. My mouth is dry, tongue swollen, throat closed. My whole body filled with grief and fear, no room for anything else. Later that night, I am alone in our crowded living room, surrounded by his family and our friends who live nearby while we wait for other loved ones to arrive who have been traveling all day to be with us. I feel alone, disoriented in a parallel world where time has stopped.

The motions of shared grief keep repeating as people arrive. Red, swollen eyes. Disbelief. Hug, cry. Wails. Hug, cry. I tell over and over how he fell back on the bed, "Debbie, I feel so dizzy." Each time I do, my body relives the moment his soul flew out the window. *Push, breathe, push, breathe.* Sit down. Wait for the next person to arrive, the next phone call, the next telling. The phone doesn't stop ringing as the news spreads. The ringing of phone, ringing of doorbell, constant ringing announcing death has arrived in my home.

Because Jim's father had died when Jim was twenty-six, his two younger sisters, only nine and seven at the time, viewed Jim as a father figure. One of them sits next to me, and even though she is steeped in her own grief she is worried I am not eating or drinking anything. I share with her my inability to swallow. She lovingly mashes a banana in a bowl, and like a concerned mother she tries feeding it to me—spoonfuls of nourishment and hope my body isn't ready to accept. I am shut down.

For her, I open and try, but the taste of banana makes me want to vomit. My stomach revolts, my throat clenches tightly, and I spit it into the palm of my hand.

Days pass and I eat what little I can manage—spoonfuls of soggy cereal, soft vanilla ice cream, chicken broth, marshmallows, and other things I can let dissolve into my mouth until there is almost nothing left to swallow. When I am able, when my throat opens just a little, it's never out of hunger. I eat because people are concerned, because I am rapidly losing weight as a part of me has disappeared with Jim. Food has no taste, and the lump stays in my throat for a very long time.

At work, co-workers are kind. We order lunch in and someone always orders me turkey on whole wheat because I no longer care and they know it's what I used to like. Before. Every day, the same sandwich: turkey on whole wheat. I unwrap and stare, then take a small piece of meat from between the bread and roll it around in my fingers. I put it in my mouth and show them all I am trying. It feels like cardboard on my tongue.

Everyone wants to nourish me out of love, caring, and kindness, and out of a love for Jim who they know would want me to be taken care of. And yet, I need time to be alone with my grief, with my struggle to make sense of what has happened, of my new place in the After world. I need room to not have to be anything or do anything other than what I am feeling in each moment, which drags on into whole days. Whole days with little food. I can drink water again. I am thirsty. My body needs to replenish all the water leaving through my near constant tears.

I have become a ghost of my former self, a griever in the depths of an abyss I am just beginning to navigate. I am a thirty-six year-old, shattered woman, now a widow. I ache for him so much my bones hurt.

I rarely accept dinner invitations with friends, and I want people to stop coming over to check on me. I am grateful for their love and concern but I want to be alone. Sometimes I say yes to keep family and friends from worrying, but I only want to be home. It's hard enough to go through the motions of life each day. Some days I don't get out of bed. But most days, I get up, get dressed, take the train to work, do my job, try to smile when my co-workers are so kind. All I really want is to crawl into bed and take an Ambien and sink into the missing of Jim.

One night, knowing I need to eat something, but with an appetite for nothing, I make cinnamon toast. For some reason, cinnamon toast is just right. I toast the bread dark, coat it with lots of butter that melts into the hot bread, and add mounds of cinnamon sugar. It isn't too much food for a stomach already stuffed with grief.

I eat this simple meal of cinnamon toast almost every night for the next month. Like a ritual, I sit and look at the two slices of buttered toast for a few moments because I'm never hungry. The smell of cinnamon and butter and sugar encourages my desire to pick up a piece and take a small bite. I chew and chew because I need to break it down so I can swallow.

I can smell the cinnamon and this is why it appeals to me. I am disconnected from everything and my senses are dulled, but the smell of cinnamon begins to lure me back because it smells like comfort. This is how I begin to eat again.

It is still hard to swallow.

Our Grieving Body

Do you know about the innate fight, flight, or freeze response? It's a physiological reaction inherited from our ancestors thousands of years ago. When we experience a shock or traumatic event, our instinctive survival responses take over. This is why, in the midst of a crisis, we are unable to eat, or swallow, or we throw up. When our brains perceive danger it instructs the body to rid itself of anything not needed to survive, preparing us to fight or run or freeze.

All energy is directed solely to survival—digestion slows down or stops and we even stop producing saliva. It's why I couldn't swallow and had no appetite.

For many of us, the acute grief and intense fear we experience keeps our bodies in continuous survival mode. This feeling may last a long time. It may be days, weeks, or months. There is no timetable. Every person's experience is unique to them. It's completely normal. We are wired to have this response.

for you

Although loved ones may worry about you, be kind to yourself. You may lose weight, or you may gain weight because all you want is ice cream. It's okay. There is no right or wrong way. Ice cream may be all you can manage to swallow for a while. It may be the only thing that comforts you. For me, it was cinnamon toast. And marshmallow fluff spooned out of the jar—it was soft and easy to swallow.

Be as good to yourself as you possibly can... even the smallest thing can make a difference... whatever that may be and whatever feels right to you.

What's your "cinnamon toast"? What brings you comfort? Even if it's hard to do in this moment, try to think of one or two things. It may not be food. Maybe it's a warm bath or a favorite soft blanket wrapped around you. Maybe it's his or her favorite tee shirt that you like to wear. I slept in one of Jim's tee shirts every night for a very long time.

All tracks vanished; you said "Travel on"
I turned to beg you stay; you had gone.
Winds pressed round me, that smelled of you
Small flowers blossomed, words from your mouth.

— *Rumi (translated by Andrew Harvey)*

~ 6 ~

Rites and Rituals

The cemetery becomes my church.

I stop going to St. Mary's on Sundays because every time I do, I start silently sobbing in the shiny brown pews where I used to sit beside Jim. The mass seems even longer, and parishioners glance over at my grief with whispers and pity, quickly glancing and then looking away. One Sunday, as the cantor sings Jim's favorite hymn "Be Not Afraid," my body shudders with the pain of trying to hold in grief so others won't stare. After that, the cemetery becomes my sacred place where I can be alone with God, Jim, and Grief.

The cemetery was already familiar. I'd often visit the family grave with Jim and his mom in springtime.

We'd plant lavender and pink and white impatiens around the headstones in memory of his father, her husband, and his paternal grandparents. The gravesite was carefully chosen for the towering oak and maple trees behind it, ensuring privacy from other graves. We picked up stray sticks and leaves to put in the trash on our way back to the car. Now I look back and think I was in training.

Sitting at the grave, moments from the day of Jim's funeral play over and over in my mind:

It was Friday, the fifth day in my new world of After. The torrential rain and slippery mud mirrored my own loose, wet body. Everything was so wet the burial service could not be held graveside. Instead, it was held inside the small chapel at the cemetery. Catholics have a funeral mass at church, followed by the Rite of Committal at the open grave.

I could see the gravesite from a chapel window, the fresh mounds of wet brown earth by the empty hole in the ground. No brightly colored impatiens blooming in late fall. Gold and orange autumn leaves fell with the rain. I asked to go out to look at the grave, even though the torrents of rain continued and it was muddy and wet and the service was about to start. Someone dissuaded me and led me back to my seat near the casket. It was time for this final act of burying my husband. Thinking of Jim's body in the casket going into that dark hole made me dizzy, and a wave of weakness washed over my body, leaving me boneless.

Earlier that morning, during the funeral at St. Mary's, I struggled to inhale. I stood in the vestibule of the church, where Jim and I stood the day we married. Now all the same friends and family were here inside waiting for us again. Now it was me walking behind him in his coffin. *Oh God, give me strength.* The cantor began to sing "Ave Maria."

I could not look up. I didn't want to see it. The music coming out of the church moved through my skin, my pores, and finally I had to look up and there it was. The mahogany casket with a blanket of white lilies. A glow of warm, soft light from the burning candles. A forest of flowered wreaths. I began to walk, with Jim's brother on one side of me and his mother on the other, but I was still alone—my lungs forgetting how to fully inhale. Small, shallow, barely alive breaths got me through the funeral.

And then a hush as we walked—despite the music, despite the throaty sobs of those who also loved Jim.

The hush of hundreds of people holding their breath, not exhaling—hundreds of wet faces, swollen red eyes staring back at us walking, and me not feeling connected to their eyes, their sorrow, to anything. I am numb, trying to stay strong, be strong for Jim, I told myself, over and over as my legs shook with the gust of grief, stomach aching, and the solitary sheath of separateness started to enfold me even though there were rows and rows of people surrounding me, overflowing from the pews of the church.

The hundreds of grievers who were seated now stood as we walk. A touching tribute to my marvelous man, my beloved, beloved by many others.

The rain, so much rain that day, mirroring our collective grief.

***

And now, here I am at his grave, reliving these moments. Walking over and over behind his casket in my mind as I stand in front of the headstone, staring at his name engraved in the marble. James R., third in line to the left. The chiseled dates telling a story of a life that ended too soon. Yes, visits to the cemetery are my ritual;

this is my sanctuary.

The ritual begins as I cry my way along the Long Island Expressway, in the early morning hours before traffic is heavy, playing music we both like. Choosing songs that connect us to each other: "Linger" by The Cranberries; Peter Gabriel: *days pass and this emptiness fills my heart;* The Counting Crows: *so when you coming home sweet angel;* and Neil Young's "Harvest Moon," a song we danced to in our living room two weeks before he died.

> Because I'm still in love with you
> I want to see you dance again
> Because I'm still in love with you
> On this harvest moon.
>
> When we were strangers
> I watched you from afar
> When we were lovers
> I loved you with all my heart.

Jim had said he would sing these words to me when we were too old to dance.

It is winter and freezing as I stand in front of the

headstone. The cold wind burns my cheeks, my eyelashes freeze from tears, and I stand in the middle of the iciness of winter, wrapped up in thick sweaters, coats and scarves, but my face, ears, fingers and toes are numb despite the layers. I want to feel it, to feel something, anything besides grief. I am alone with the cold and icy wind, alone with Jim, and I feel his presence, wondering if he can feel what I feel, the hollowness of our separation. I pray to God for meaning, for understanding, for mercy.

I stay as long as I can, until I can't feel my lips, until I run out of tissues to catch my dripping nose. Only then do I return to the car, turn on the heat and sit there with the engine on, hot air melting the cold in my body, me melting with the heat, all of my body melting with the grief until I am almost too tired to drive home.

I repeat this almost every weekend—the drive, the songs, the bitter cold, the thawing out in the car. Sometimes I go twice a week. I go to feel connected to him in a tangible way. The visits permeate the fogginess of my abyss.

One afternoon in Penn Station, I see Jim. The back of his head. My heart pounds against the cage of my chest to be let out. I think, *I knew it, I knew he wouldn't leave me.* I see him other places, too, in cafes, on city streets, so many times, until the head turns or I run up to a stranger's face and startle them with the hope in mine.

So I go to the cemetery to keep it real. This sacred space is helping me to transition to the world of After. The towering trees, sentinels sheltering the grave, whisper comfort with the wind, their changing leaves gently showing me time is moving forward. *Time is moving forward.*

Even though I talk to Jim all the time, I go to the cemetery to feel a deeper connection as every day I'm learning again how to say good-bye. I know he is watching me. He is part of this ritual. A communion between us exists, and I know it always will.

Beginning to Navigate the Labyrinth of Loss

Funerals and other ways of honoring the loss of loved ones are tremendously difficult. At the time, I felt I had to behave in a certain way to accommodate cultural expectations. I did my best but every person is different. I know I couldn't have done it without all the support surrounding me. Know this: you do what you can. Don't worry about pleasing other people or doing something that doesn't feel right to you. Someone who's been through this said, "Do what you need to do, even if it means not doing what you're supposed to do."

Joan Didion wrote The Year of Magical Thinking after her husband's death. The first months often have "magical thinking," with a part of you not fully able to absorb the fact that your loved one is really gone and is not coming back. You keep hoping and wishing and denying. In the beginning, in the hazy few moments of waking, I'd keep my eyes closed and reach my left arm to feel his side of the bed, praying, please let him be there.

If this is your experience, know it will pass eventually. There will come a time when your psyche has fully absorbed the loss and the "magical thinking" will ease. It doesn't mean you will stop wishing it weren't true.

When Jim first died, my Great Aunt Olga told me the pain doesn't go away, but you will learn how to live with it. This has been my experience. Other people have a different experience, telling me the pain does go away. For some, like me, it does not. It lessens, it integrates, and you learn how to live with it. It does not mean you have not healed, it means you've healed as much as you can. Everyone experiences loss in their own way. People love differently, heal differently, feel differently, cope differently.

Grieving is complicated. It's like a maze. You go back and forth, sometimes surprised to find yourself almost back where you started. So you take another step and start another path through the maze. You'll try this way or that way until you find the way right for you. You may not see the end yet, the way out yet, but know it is there. The only way out of grief is to go through it.

My ritual of going to the cemetery continued for a long time. Eventually I moved back to the city and my visits became less frequent. The tears became different over time, softer, less harsh, and sorrow began to move into the place where grief had lived. I felt guilty about this and had to remind myself that Jim would want this. I knew I didn't need to go to his grave to communicate with him, just as I knew I didn't have to go to church to communicate with God.

I still miss Jim, and this is okay. It doesn't mean I'm not happy, it doesn't mean I'm dwelling in the past, and it doesn't mean I'm not living a full and meaningful life. It means my heart will always carry the wound of losing him. And this is okay. As much as I believe he lives on in spirit and our souls don't die, as often as I feel his presence, I am a human being having a human experience. And so are you.

for you

We all form our own rituals, our own way of handling what's been handed to us. What helps you to feel connected to your loved one? Is there something you shared together that you both enjoyed? Is it music? Walks in nature? Gardening?

Maybe you plant a tree. Or visit the cemetery every week, like I did for almost a year. You can create a scrapbook with photos and mementos. Reread cards and letters while playing a special song. Donate to a charity in their memory.

Carry something special that reminds you of them, like a stone or shell. My cousin started a grief center in memory of her daughter.

You'll find your own rituals that offer you comfort, offer you a way of coping, offer you a path to healing. You don't have to explain or rationalize; you do what feels right for you. Whatever helps get you through.

"The darker the night, the brighter the stars,
The deeper the grief, the closer is God!"

— *Fyodor Dostoyevsky*

~ 7 ~

Walking the Stairs

It is cold and dark in the weeks and winter months following Jim's death. The sun sets before 5 p.m., enveloping me in a darkness I feel even during the day. I return to my job, even though my boss insists I take as much time as I need. I don't know what else I need, but I know I need a reason to get out of bed. Time seems to stretch endlessly ahead without Jim to witness life with me.

Getting out of bed to go to work is a daily challenge. Some mornings I can't, but most days it's the only reason I do. It connects me with something other than my own solitary existence. It takes me out of the bottomless grief and into the world of stocks and bonds and other people interacting, where I am still Debbie, the securities trader.

Where I have a purpose, where I still have part of my old identity. It is familiar and helps me keep one foot in reality, connecting me with something so I don't float away.

Each morning I awake from the fog of Ambien-induced sleep. My first feeling is searing pain from the awareness Jim is no longer beside me and I begin a strange negotiation game with myself with the goal of finishing all the mundane tasks that seem insurmountable. Every little thing takes so much effort. To get myself from the bed to the bathroom I tell myself, *just pee, then you can go back to bed.* While I am up, I tell myself, *c'mon Debbie, if you can pee you can brush your teeth.* In this way, I egg myself on, negotiating with the pain and always allowing myself the fallback option: *you can always go back to bed.* The anguish engulfs me, sheathing me in my solitary world of in-between, of pleading for Before and resisting the world of After. Most days I manage to walk out the front door, bargaining with each next step until I am finally at my desk.

Every morning I take the Long Island Railroad from Manhasset to Penn Station, the many bodies standing on the train platform in black wool coats with *Wall Street Journal*s or *The New York Times* tucked under their arms and steam rising from morning coffee. I stare at the clusters of men and women waiting for the train, looking at them through the thick lens of my shock. All of them robotic, all their heads turning to look down tracks—here comes the train, doors open, they all step on the train. Hundreds of men and women, hundreds of briefcases. *Don't they know that Jim has died? Don't they know everything has changed?* I want to scream, but instead I look down the tracks with them for the oncoming train. When the doors open I also step inside. Going through the motions of life. I don't have to feel alive in those motions. I just have to do what everyone else is doing. Following along, surrounded by the invisible fog only I feel. This is how I get to work.

But then I have to return home.

I am greeted by the cold and dark as the train drops me back into my town, and by the end of the day my legs feel as if there are ten-pound weights attached to each ankle, laden with sadness. I arrive home and stare at the white front door. Sometimes for twenty minutes. Sometimes longer. Standing in ice-cold air, not caring that on the other side is heat, not wanting to open that door to the emptiness of my life inside.

Just weeks before, I opened the door easily, fueled by the imagination that Jim would be there. The light would be on and when I stepped inside I'd see him coming down the stairs to greet me with a hug, a kiss, wanting to know about my day. The days have passed and my ability to imagine this has begun to fade. Now I stand at the door and it is difficult to put my key in the lock and push it open.

Once inside, I close the door behind me and lean against it, my back still wanting to be somewhere else, my heart facing the stairs that lead me to this home that is still my home, minus Jim. I stay against the door, inside, gloves still on my hands, and a scarf wrapped around my face, snow caked on the soles of my boots turning into a puddle around me. In the dark, in my foyer, not turning on the light. Silence, silence, silence, my knees weakening at the entrance and my legs trembling. Wanting to scream again, not accepting how my life could be so altered.

Night after night, in the foyer of my home, broken. Wondering how he could leave me, wondering how a heart endures this much, cloaked in not only winter clothes, but also in my solitary anguish. I surrender to self-pity and sorrow, and eventually my small body that feels so heavy somehow makes it up the stairs to the living room.

And yet here I am again, in the foyer, and I can't do it this time. I can't walk up those stairs. I let my legs stop doing their job, and they softly, quietly collapse on the cold tile floors of my home. The stairs are my Everest, and my legs can't make it to the summit. They give up. Eventually my whole body gives up until my ear and cheek are pressed against the cold tile floor. Even my fingers and toes are crying, the way I did during those first days. The heaving sobs hurt my ribs, my stomach, my lungs, my throat. Animal sounds. Tears in my hair, wet face against tile floor. The sobbing that comes from the soul of a woman without.

Lying on the floor, I go from hopelessness to rage. Rage fills my entire body, consuming me with its power. I start with God, accusing him, then I go onto Jim, the whole world, then beyond the world we know, and I rage at the unknown, too—the whole unseen universe. As the rage intensifies my cries are harder and louder and I question my faith, everything I believe about life, love, humanity. *What kind of God are you?* I accuse. *Don't you know what kind of life I had and how with Jim I finally found safety? How could you take him away from me? You are not a good and loving God!!*

I rage until the rage scares me with its potency, and when I am finished I only feel more alone and more abandoned. Yet, through my rage, there is a part of me that knows God does not have a personal vendetta against me and that Jim did not want to leave. My rage is ancient and my behavior a way to protect my tender heart holding hurts not fully healed from other wounds. All of those wounds are with me now, opened again.

From rage I go into despair, still on the floor, still crying. This familiar place, reminiscent of my teen years when I lay on the floor of my bedroom wondering how much more a young girl could take in one lifetime. And then a thought creeps in.

I don't want to do this anymore. I can't do this anymore. I am done.

I begin to hear in my voice now the sound of a prayer, reaching back out to the same God I had just given up on, hoping He would listen. *Please, God, let me die tonight. Right now. I have no more strength. I'm empty and ready. Please take me.*

All I hear is silence as I wait. Waiting to die. Wanting to die. Easier to die than face walking up those stairs one more time to the lonely bedroom where a bottle of sleeping pills are waiting for me in the drawer of the night stand on my side of the bed. I can take that whole bottle and never have to face the stairs again.

You can always go back to bed.

In the stillness of waiting, I suddenly feel God beside me, and Jim too. In the long silence, in the quiet of the moments following my raging storm, a message comes through with clarity.

Taking your life is not the answer. Think of all the people who love you. How could you do this to them? Do you want to cause others the tremendous pain you are suffering now? This is not the answer, not the way. You are surrounded by love. Taking your life would not honor Jim.

I know it is a message from God, from Jim, from Divine Spirit.

I lift my head off the tile floor and look around me. It is all true, this message. Jim would hate for me to be this miserable. Slowly I begin to lift my body with both palms pressed against the cold tile.

To honor Jim for the man he was and the love we shared means not hurting myself and not wanting to die. I know this with certainty as soon as the message comes through. To honor him would be to get up off the cold floor and walk up those stairs.

And I do.

Indeed, it may take years
to realize that what was calamitous at the time
was instrumental in your spiritual growth.
The wound is the place where the light enters you.

— *Rumi (translated by Andrew Harvey)*

The Grace of Darkness

There is a place of darkness that so many of us have known or may be experiencing right now. We feel so alone and every single thing is an effort. We feel hopeless. I've been in that place, as have so many others. I've had clients come in wondering if the despair and bleak hopelessness will ever abate. If you're feeling this way now, know that this feeling, this dark place, is a natural part of the grieving process. To feel angry, to rage at your loved one, at God, at the world, the universe, is completely natural.

Many of us have other losses we may still be grieving, even if it's from a very long time ago. A life-altering loss like losing someone you love can trigger the hurt and trauma from these older losses, impacting and magnifying our current grief. It can bring up many unresolved "wounds of the heart" and draw you even deeper into despair. This is something to be aware of and another reason to seek professional help if you feel overwhelmed by this.

If you are in this dark place, I urge you, with all my heart, to find someone who can help you. I wholehearted-ly believe in therapy; it was crucial to my healing. I became a therapist because I wanted to help others like my therapist helped me. If therapy is not an option for you, I urge you to reach out to someone who will help you through this dark peri-od. Find someone you can trust, who will hold you when you are in such pain. If you go to a place of worship, reach out to your pastor, your priest, your rabbi. Find a support group, call a hotline, your best friend, a family member—call someone you know can hold you through this time. I urge you, if you're in this place, just hold on, breathe through it, cry through it, for these moments pass, and you WILL get through it.

This night on the floor was a turning point for me. Receiving this message let a small ray of light into the dark-ness I felt. It was a shift to a different type of experience. It was what manifested my wholeness into a new normal—a transformative spiritual awakening. It shifted my view of my spirituality, my beliefs, and deepened my sense of connection to something much bigger than me. It deepened my connec-tion to Jim. I had gone to therapy to help with my grieving, and this night changed the therapy process for me. It allowed me to step out of the solitary and fully welcome the many hearts waiting for me.

Moments like this often carry a possibility of new understanding or spiritual awakening. When you're at your lowest point—the lowest imaginable—this is when you can actually have a life-changing and transformative spiritual experience.

At the bottom of the stairs was my own "dark night of the soul." One we all experience at some point in our lives. It's in this moment, this space, that it's possible to be touched by grace. It opens possibilities for Spirit to reach you when you are at the bottom of the well. For it's when we hit bottom that we need grace most.

God, Divine Love, Divine Spirit, whatever name you use, is always present. Let it cradle you, and let yourself be given the gift of having insight, feeling a blessing of peace. It's an expanded sphere of spirituality. If you are religious, you can still have religion as your anchor, but you can expand your being to the things that give you solace, all while connected to a sense of spirituality and unity.

for you

If you've been in this dark place you know what it's like. If you're in it, if you feel hopeless, I urge you to reach out to someone who cares and let them help you. Let them help you grieve. Let them listen to your anger. It will get better. It just takes time. Write a letter to your loved one, to God, to the Universe, filling it with all your anger.

There WILL be a moment you will move to the other side of grief. It could be in your darkest moment, just as it was for me. You will feel the shift; you will know it. You'll hear the sounds of life again, feel the wind, breathe in a sunny day, something will happen and the awareness of the shift will be clear. Like having lived through a very long storm and then one morning the sun comes out.

I remember feeling the wind wrap around me on a walk one day and thinking it was Jim's way of giving me a hug. I've carried this feeling all these years—it's why I love the wind. I remember that moment so clearly, for I felt the connection to him so strongly. And I still do, every time.

Keep a small journal with you. Whenever it occurs to you what might honor the memory of your loved one, write it down. Maybe you're already in that space, tending their garden, giving to a charity, continuing something they began. Write it down. You'll be glad you did as you continue to heal.

Remember,
the entrance door to the sanctuary is inside you.

— *Rumi (translated by Andrew Harvey)*

~ 8 ~

Lost

My body wants to move. It is a couple of months after Jim died and a new ritual begins. I get up and walk every night in the cold night air. If it's snowing or too cold I walk on the treadmill in the small study off the bedroom. I walk to shake off the heavy cloak of shock that has begun to lighten. I walk to leave the thick fog of sorrow behind. I walk toward and I walk away.

I walk to stay in between moments because it's hard to stay in one feeling. If I stop moving, the world of After will catch up with me, so I walk as a way to cope with the struggle of acceptance, as a way to exhaust myself into sleep.

I can't stand to be in my skin. I can't stand to be at home. I can't stand to be with people. I can't stand to be alone. I can't stand being.

I walk fast with headphones on my ears, the volume turned up high, music drowning out the feelings and thoughts. I carry just the house key. The music has to be hard, pounding rock: Guns and Roses, Led Zeppelin and The Cult. Songs I play over and over like *"Sweet Child O' Mine"* and *"Fire Woman."* I am a woman on fire and the lyrics speak to me.

Fire, smoke she is a rising, as I walk past the homes with families inside, moving to family rhythms. *Fire, yeah, some on the horizon,* as I walk past green trash cans and black cats who I let cross my path, because what do I have to lose?

The loud music shakes my senses and matches the level of anxiety living in my body. *Fire, oh smoke stack lightning, smoke stack lightning.*

I don't play soft, slow music or anything Jim and I both liked.

One night, lost in the pounding bass and the lyrics and the too-fast walking, not paying attention to street signs, whether I am turning left or right, I walk so far past our own neighborhood that I stop and suddenly realize nothing is familiar.

It's been so hard to focus or concentrate these past few months, and tonight is no exception. The homes aren't familiar, the street name—Walnut Lane—unfamiliar, and I have no phone. It's just me, standing still and not recognizing anything. Lost with no phone, just my feet, my music, my key, and my desire to walk right out of this new life without Jim and back into my old life.

I know the houses of our neighborhood well and these aren't those houses. I remember when Jim and I walked after dinner to our favorite streets, with our favorite houses, dreaming of the time we could afford to buy our own. Maybe on Eakins Road or Ryder Road, but we never came to a Walnut Lane.

It's dark and late and I'm tired and sweating. I take the headphones off my ears and the pounding music turns into the still silence of late night. It's then, in the quiet, I notice I've walked right out of one season and into another. It's an unusually warm early spring night, and there are buds forming on the bare branches of the trees. I see the moon has moved in the sky since I left home hours earlier.

I stand on the corner, not sure which way to go, and I take in the silence of the night, everyone tucked into their beds, rows and rows of families now quiet, and I feel an emptiness inside and connect with a place music cannot reach.

I am lost.

No cars pass me, and most homes are completely dark. I become angry. First at myself for not paying attention to where I was going, and then at Jim for not being at home to worry about me, to miss me, to come and find me.

In an instant my anger turns to fear as the reality of my situation sinks in. I have no phone, no money and nobody knows where I am. I feel lost in the wilderness with only the moon and stars as my guide.

Which way do I go? With the music off, I walk with my thoughts and with all my senses heightened. I am living in a dark place, lost in my new world of After. I don't know where I belong or how I fit into the world anymore without Jim.

Now I see a familiar house, a large grey one with black shutters, set back on a big lawn with an old graceful tree guarding the sleeping people inside. It's on a corner I've driven past before. Relief floods my body. How far have I gone? Far enough for the moon to hang even lower in the sky.

By the time I find my way home, I am exhausted. The thoughts that accompanied me come to bed with me. I lay there with blistered feet and legs weak from miles of walking and think no matter how hard or how far I walk, the grief is still with me. No matter what I do to escape, it won't go away. It's lying by my side, telling me I have to slow down enough to go through it, to face it straight on. I begin to cry and surrender.

The Fog Lifts and Surrender Begins

When the shock and numbness begin to wear off, reality starts to sink in around the edges. When it happens is different for everyone. Sometimes it's a few weeks, sometimes it's a few months. There is no timetable. Almost everyone experiences anxiety. There are many ways we try to alleviate it. For me, it was walking. What is it for you? It could be binge watching Netflix or drinking too much or eating too much or sleeping too much or cleaning the house over and over or keeping yourself so busy you don't have to time to think. That's the whole point—it's hard to be in the new world of After.

I channeled my anxiety into walking. Although I didn't know it then, now I know the compulsive walking and the feeling of not wanting to be in my body was an unconscious way of trying to avoid feeling the deeper grief that follows shock. The grief you feel when the fog lifts.

When Jim died I didn't know any other young widows. After 9/11, when I knew so many, too many widows, I discovered I could help those who were now going through something I knew about. I found I could offer comfort and be with them, holding a space that many have never known. Holding their gaze in a way people couldn't hold mine when I was a new widow.

And I would ask some of them, "Do you sometimes feel like you can't stand to be in your skin?" And the astonishment in their pain filled eyes, as they said, "Yes, how did you know? I thought I was the only one."

So if this is your experience, know this: you are not the only one. You're not going crazy.

I had to stop the "magical thinking" and face the fact that this WAS my life now. And I could either keep walking, or start the deeper grieving of acceptance so I could find my way back. This is how I began to heal.

That dark night of being lost helped guide the way for me to walk into the world of After, into my new life, my new normal. Remember, grief is not linear. You will go back and forth between all the phases of anger and denial and bargaining and depression and acceptance. Sometimes in one day. Sometimes in one hour. So as you stumble and stride and stop to gather strength along the way towards healing, be compassionate toward yourself.

for you

Meditation is a wonderful way to ground and come back to your body. It helps to calm you and releases tension and anxiety. I know it may be too difficult in the beginning stages of healing to do it for very long. But even a few deep breaths help during anxious moments.

Walking is a form of meditation and a great way to release anxiety. You'll find yourself developing a rhythm, left, right, left, right, as you breathe. Please bring your cell phone. If you go for a walk in nature (which is wonderfully soothing) let someone know where you're going and when you'll return.

Can I see another's woe,
And not be in sorrow too?
Can I see another's grief,
And not seek for kind relief?

— *William Blake*

~ 9 ~

Crossing the Street

I see Dan before he sees me. I am walking along Main Street in our small suburban town on my way to the stationery store to buy thank you cards. It is a cold winter morning, and I am walking with the tide of people, on a Saturday, at a Saturday pace, with no pounding music in my ears, flanked by the leafless winter trees in late morning sun. Jim has been dead for a few months and winter is my shroud.

Dan is less than two blocks away, his bright red parka contrasting with the piles of grey snow lining the sidewalks. I see him look up as he shifts his gaze from the sidewalk to my eyes. In that instant of recognition, I lift my hand to wave to him, but he is already looking back down at the pavement and stops walking. He turns to his right, looks both ways, and crosses the street. Away from me, away from the reminder I represent that his close friend is dead, pretending not to see me.

Dan cries every time he sees me or talks to me on the phone. Other people do, too, but for Dan it cuts deeper and seeing me reminds him of his own terrible grief, and he has trouble moving beyond it. I stand there on this cold winter day and watch him cross the street. I feel rejected. When people see me in the post office, at the stores in our town, on the train going to and from work, they don't see me as Debbie. I feel like they see me as the woman who carries grief with her and might pass it on to them like a disease.

And so I stand here, on the central street in this small town, watching Dan's red parka disappear into his safe place where grief won't touch him this Saturday morning. I stand on the cold concrete, holding my grief and his grief too. I feel sorrow for his sadness. I under-stand my presence can make others uncomfortable. Instead of seeing me, they see what can so easily happen to them too. This awareness doesn't make it any easier.

Later, at home, I think of how difficult it is for

some people to look into my eyes because they might see a woman trying to hold bits and pieces of herself together. For some, my eyes might reflect back the kind of pain they cannot bear to see.

The avalanche of calls, the letters, the "what can I dos" have slowed. No longer a tsunami of grief, but still a wave powerful enough to knock me over and take my breath away. I'm getting used to whispers and averted eyes. *That's her, she's the one whose husband died in her arms, he was only 45.*

I am walking with a huge hole in my life, and I'm not walking alone. I am walking with all the others who are grieving too—widows, children, parents, friends, and siblings.

I have to remember that Dan is walking the walk of grief his own way, too. Sometimes this walk means avoiding the pain and crossing the street.

I go to a friend's house later that afternoon, a friend who can hold my gaze and has the strength to look at all of it with me, who lets me tell the same story over and over, and doesn't pretend I'm not there.

As You Begin To Heal

When life returns to its normal pace, when people see you weeks and months later, your presence may remind them that normal life doesn't always continue the same way indefinitely. They may not know what to say to you, as Dan didn't know what to say to me—they may even avoid you.

It's hard to face our own mortality, to face the fact we will all lose people we love. It's hard to look at someone who's going through what may be our worst nightmare.

At first I was stunned and hurt. Eventually, I began to understand and could feel compassion. I felt sorrow for the sadness of others and sorrow for a different kind of loss for me. Knowing my presence could cause discomfort, that people were withdrawing because they didn't know what to say, was a loss for me because it hurt and because I needed support.

Let people have their space to grieve or avoid grief in their own way. Their avoidance is not about you. It's about them.

for you

If someone can't be there for you the way you need them to be, find someone who can and will.

Continue to let others help you while you take the space and time you need. As much as you can, surround yourself with those who can hold you, hug you, love you, and listen.

Debbie Augenthaler

EMERGING
and
TRANSITION

"Rarely do we realize that we
are in the midst of the extraordinary.
Miracles occur all around us,
signs from God show us the way,
angels plead to be heard.."

— *Paulo Coelho*

~ 10 ~

Gift of Permission

I have survived a whole year of firsts, and acceptance is dragging me reluctantly into the second year. My wings still feel broken and shriveled, my shoulder blades still hunched over in self-protection. I have accepted Jim is gone and yet I am worn out after a year of trying to be okay. I am able to function now, living in the world of my new normal, but I am not okay.

The holidays are approaching, and it feels like the first time without Jim. Last year they started just weeks after he died, when I was still in shock. I decide to spend Thanksgiving at a retreat in the woods of California to gather my strength for Christmas. I'm not looking forward to trying to seem okay just so I don't upset everyone else.

Among the tall ponderosa pines and the crisp northern California air and the Milky Way vastness sparkling overhead I meet her—an intuitive healer at the retreat center. I know I must schedule an appointment with her when I first see her glide across the green grass as if she isn't from Earth. Twenty minutes into our time together I know why. Her soft hand gently reaches for mine when the tremors of grief and the tears distract me from her dark, penetrating eyes. She whispers words of wisdom and knowing to the part of me waiting for permission—something I didn't know I was seeking. But she knew. Her long, black hair brushes against my arm as she comes to sit by my side. Her arm is now around me, my head guided to rest on her shoulder as my own shoulders shake and I sob. She gives me the gift of permission to be exactly where I am right now with my grief.

She tells me I need time to cocoon. She calls me "dear" and tells me to take as long as I need. My weary, wet eyes look into her strong, dry ones when she tells me I will emerge from this experience not just a survivor, but stronger, brighter, and more beautiful than ever—like a butterfly. She promises me this, and her knowing of the future helps me hold onto the hope this is possible, even if I can't see what she sees.

Before her comforting words I felt like I was failing a societal rulebook for grieving, like I was supposed to be stronger. I had to be reminded that real strength grows out of weakness. Her gentle wisdom gives me permission to be okay with my feelings. I am still in need of tremendous healing. I am tender, vulnerable, and raw. And this is okay.

After her words, my shoulders straighten a little. I feel a gentle tingling as hope pulls like a thin thread on my dormant wings.

She is one of my angels. Angels have been coming to me in all forms. Now, I am beginning to pay attention when they arrive.

You Make the Rules

All the "firsts" are difficult. Sometimes the anticipation of the holidays or special days like birthdays and anniversaries are more upsetting than the actual event itself. They are a marker, a reminder, a way of reinforcing the reality that the person you love is really not coming back. As time goes on, acceptance comes in, but it doesn't take away the wish that it wasn't true.

Everyone is different, but for me, it took a long time for the shock to wear off and to accept my new reality. And so when the first-year markers began to turn into the second ones, they felt like firsts for me, as I no longer had the numbness of shock to buffer the strain of the holidays.

I felt I was supposed to be further along in my grieving because it had been a year. Not that people said this directly, but I know they thought it. This is not a criticism. If you've never suffered a devastating loss you can't know how it feels—

even though everyone will at some point in their lives. I felt like I was failing an unwritten rulebook of grief: wow, it's been a year already and you're still so steeped in it?

I was exhausted from trying to hold back my feelings so as not to make others uncomfortable. I was lucky to have the support of close loved ones and my therapist, but even so, I felt self-conscious and thought I was never going to feel okay again. Many of my clients have felt this way, and you might be feeling it, too. You will feel better, but you need to take the time you need. It's okay to not be okay. And if you're feeling much better, that's okay, too. There is no rulebook! Remember, grief is not linear, and there is no timetable.

The wise woman's words planted a seed of hope by using a metaphor I could understand. A caterpillar's world is turned upside down, literally—it hangs from a twig or leaf and spins a cocoon, or molts into a chrysalis. Once it's safely encased, the caterpillar digests itself, dissolving all its tissues. But the cells, the essence of the caterpillar, remain and reassemble, developing into a butterfly. When the transformation is complete, the butterfly emerges from the chrysalis. It's amazing to watch. The butterfly is tentative at first, hanging upside down, letting its wilted wings dry and begin to firm. Then its wings start to flutter, and eventually it gains the strength to fly away.

for you

Your world has been turned upside down.

Take the time you need to cocoon.

Be patient with yourself.

Do what you need to do as you heal.

And look for the angels in your life.

The Thing Is
by Ellen Bass

to love life, to love it even
when you have no stomach for it
and everything you've held dear
crumbles like burnt paper in your hands,
your throat filled with the silt of it.
When grief sits with you, its tropical heat
thickening the air, heavy as water
more fit for gills than lungs;
when grief weights you like your own flesh
only more of it, an obesity of grief,
you think, How can a body withstand this?
Then you hold life like a face
between your palms, a plain face,
no charming smile, no violet eyes,
and you say, yes, I will take you
I will love you, again.

Debbie Augenthaler

And entering with relief some quiet place
Where never fell his foot or shone his face
I say, "There is no memory of him here!"
And so stand stricken, so remembering him.

— *Edna St. Vincent Millay*

~ 11 ~

It's Hard To Let Go

I count each day for one hundred days and then I stop counting. I suffer through the holidays, the anniversaries, the changing seasons, and even the anniversary of his death. Days slip and slide together into the murkiness of grief until a whole year has passed.

Everyone tells me to wait a year before making big decisions, so just after a year I sell our townhouse in Manhasset near the Long Island Railroad tracks, where everything went right and then everything went wrong. It was the neighborhood where Jim and I dreamt of buying a home. After dinner, we would walk past New England style houses, including one with black shutters, an old stone chimney, and a cherry red door that beckoned us to open it and walk into our future.

When I sell the townhouse, I walk away from everything that might have been behind that cherry red door of our dreams. Living in the suburbs represented everything I could no longer have without Jim. Families with laughing, adorable children running around in the streets, on the sidewalks, at the high school track where I liked to walk on windy days. I didn't want to mask the anger mixed with sadness simmering inside me that I would never have this with Jim. I knew I stood out here, representing something dark and scary about life that people wanted to push out of their consciousness, feeling like I was wearing a sign announcing "Widow Walking."

I'm selling a home that held a life that was no longer mine, and yet when our home goes into contract, I feel like my skin is being pulled off my body. I walk through every room of our home the night before the closing, into all the spaces that held our memories, to touch it, witness it one more time. I walk by the elegant, dark furniture Jim preferred over my more whimsical taste and feel the weight of the dark wood and graceful chairs. I walk by the buffet holding our wedding china, with the large, heavy, wood-framed mirror centered above.

Jim liked things that matched and went well together. He liked order. When we worked together, I'd wait until he stepped away and then open his desk drawer with all the pens and pencils neatly arranged and mess them, making both of us laugh. When we lived together I'd tease him about how well he organized files with bills and statements and documents. He'd laugh and say, "Debbie, I know you're secretly on your knees thanking me for this." He was right. I hated doing paperwork and paying bills, and after he died, I hated it even more.

Jim and I were different—he was more traditional and went for classic furniture made of heavy wood with brass handles, while I gravitated toward "shabby chic." Jim grew up in a warm, inviting home, the kind we dreamed of owning, while my design imprint involved military housing, small apartments, and even a trailer. After my father left when I was a young girl, all of our furniture was second hand or donated, chipped or broken in some way. A mirroring of how I was broken when I met Jim.

Now, on this last night in the townhouse, my hands longingly pass over the furniture Jim had chosen, that spoke of home, safety, family, and grounding. All the things I never had and all the things Jim and this home gave me. I suddenly feel this life we built was a cosmic joke. Rumblings of old hurts merging with new ones spark flames of anger and sorrow.

I walk into our bedroom for the last time. I look at our bed piled with matching shams and pillows and all the memories—Jim putting his lips on my neck and his hands on my hips— past the antique pine armoire to the pine chest with the leaning mirror—where I could see him watching me get ready for work. The bedroom was no longer a safe space. Creamy lampshades with a soft glow, as I move through memories of both love and death.

Going back down the stairs, my hands on the banister, I feel all of it, the love and the disagreements. The long walks planning our futures now lodged in my feet and inside my thighs. The baby we didn't have in my aching womb. Holding Jim that fateful morning now heavy in my arms. I am leaving this home behind but the memories are gathered in the house of my body.

I sit down on the stairs I couldn't walk up after he died and grieve the life no longer mine to live.

I move back to Manhattan and watch planes take off and land at LaGuardia from the small balcony of the 18th floor. Wishing I was on one of them. It isn't the home

Jim and I dreamt of at all. It's a one bedroom, one bath, with a small extra room off the kitchen. The smallness of it reflects the new size of my life. It's close enough to the Triboro Bridge that still connects me to my old life to visit friends, in-laws, his children, and his grave.

I buy new furniture. It isn't dark and doesn't have weight; it's a rose-colored plush sofa that Jim would have hated. I mix it with some of our old things. The newness speaks of the woman I am becoming—gone are the pictures of horses and hunting dogs and in their place is a large painting, much taller than me, of the mystical and haunting interior of a cathedral, echoing arches and altars of ancient times. I bring church home.

Part of the old is a big blue square Tiffany box I carry into the apartment myself, not entrusting it to the movers. It originally held a wedding present. The contents in the blue box are sacred. Whenever I feel disconnected from my old life, I put on one of Jim's old tee shirts, take the blue box down from the closet shelf and pour a glass of wine. I sit on the floor and tenderly pull out the items that take up space in that box: our wedding program, restaurant menus, all the many cards he'd given me over the years, Jim's memo pad where he wrote down everything we spent in neat, penciled handwriting. Even the morning coffee at Louie's before the train every morning, just to make me laugh.

Also in the box are notes he used to sneak to me at the office years earlier. Smiling as he slipped one into the palm of my hand while passing me in the halls. Paper unfolded to his neat handwriting, *Debbie, our place in an hour?* In an hour I'd find him on the steps of St. Patrick's Cathedral on Fifth Avenue, just a few blocks away but what seemed like miles from our office. It was there he first said he loved me, his voice shaking, the early morning New York street sounds muffled by my heart's wild pounding. It was there he asked me to be with him always.

The blue box and its contents drift me back into the beautiful moments of our relationship, but by the second glass of wine I lift out the funeral program and move onto the sympathy cards, donations to charities made in his honor, handwritten notes by people who wanted to tell me that Jim made a difference in their lives. Letters that made me laugh and cry, gratitude from donor recipients whose lives had been forever gifted.

It's hard to let go.

I've left our old home and the old spaces, but I

have the blue box to transport me back in time. In this way I enter my new life but still have a place where I can visit my old one when I want.

It feels freeing to be back in the city again. I like not being tied to train schedules, and relish the extra hour of sleep in the morning. After months of saying no I become the woman who says yes. Yes to dinner, drinks, concerts, and smoking cigarettes while drinking martinis in dark bars. Yes to living life on the other side of that red door.

My friends and colleagues don't know that yes is another kind of avoidance. It keeps me from the apartment, from the contents inside the blue box. Even with all the invitations, all the plays and music and drinks and conversation, I often return home, slip off the little black dress and stiletto heels and put on Jim's fraying tee shirt that now smells like me. I pour a glass of wine.

And I reach for the box. It is something I can go back to, a small anchor in an uncertain world. In the morning I wake up and begin the lessons of learning how to live again, one yes at a time.

Transition Time

Waiting a year to make any big decisions after a life-altering loss is a wise adage. It's difficult to make permanent decisions when it's hard to think clearly. I've explained the physiological effects of trauma in earlier chapters—remember, the pre-frontal cortex, the logical, thinking part of your brain isn't working optimally. If you can, wait for those big decisions until you've had some time to begin healing.

I needed to withdraw for a while, and that's okay. Not everyone does. But eventually, I was strong enough to go out and about and start living life again. I was still grieving but I was also beginning to heal. Saying yes to everything was a way of avoiding the emotions of another kind of grief, of acceptance and moving ahead. In living in your "new normal," fresh grief and mourning is natural. You are letting go of that which WAS and stepping forward into that which IS—a new way of being in the world. It is a time of transition and seesaw emotions, back and forth and up and down.

Many of us experience feelings of guilt when we begin healing. Like when I felt free after moving back to the city. I liked living in the city. Yes, I'd have given anything to be back in the suburbs with Jim, but that wasn't going to happen. And I was having fun, laughing again, and enjoying my social life. At first it was almost confusing—I'd think, how is it possible I'm enjoying anything? I'd feel guilty, and have to remind myself Jim would want me to be happy. Days when I felt good and days when I didn't—when the non-linear phases of grief would ricochet around inside me—anger, bargaining, denial (still? I'd think), the wishing and pleading—it's all part of healing. My therapist was invaluable in helping me sort out and understand these feelings.

for you

Do you have a ritual or rituals? It can be very comforting to have one that resonates with you. I bought a beautiful, large white candle especially for the firsts. And on every first—the first Christmas, his birthday, etc.—I would light it and watch it glow at night, feeling like it was a way of connecting with Jim. I'd watch the flame flicker, and imagine it was his breath making the flame dance.

Beginning to heal and adjusting to your new life doesn't mean having to let go of the person you love. Wearing his tee shirts and reading his words of love brought me a lot of comfort as I transitioned into my new life. I'd light the big white candle underneath the new painting leaning against my bedroom wall and watch the flames flicker, feeling our forever connection.

Do what feels good to you.

"Angels walk among us,
Sometimes the only thing we may not see
are the wings upon their backs."

— *Molly Fredenfield*

~ 12 ~

The Butterfly Clan

A year after I move back to the city, I gather with some of the angels in my life, in the backyard of my Great Aunt Olga's home in Tulsa, Oklahoma. We sit outside, the sun radiating on our skin as we drink red wine, some of us smoking Benson & Hedges menthol cigarettes, and we laugh at shameless stories of men, sharing ancestral stories that border on myth. We arrive from Arizona, Florida, and New York for a reunion, but we are all so close it's as if we walked down the street with our morning coffee to sit on the front steps of memory. This Easter weekend our bonds seem to transcend blood and marriage. All of us gather: Aunt Olga, Aunt Jennee, my cousins Laura and Mary, and Judy, my cousin by blood and my aunt by marriage (it's a Southern thing).

We drink expensive celebratory wine and we settle into the solidness of sisterhood. We tell the stories of our mothers and grandmothers while eating sour cream dip with Lay's potato chips, pepper jack cheese, and melting M&M's. Some of us drop ice into our wine and stir it with our fingers, watching it melt quickly in the sultry spring air, though there isn't really a spring in Oklahoma, just summer and winter. But I can smell it anyway, outside with my tribe, how the awakening of this season stretches back to ancient times. Maybe spring here happens in a day, when the rosebuds open and the air becomes thick with summer. All six of us meet on that one day, the season when everything seems possible again, sitting around the redwood picnic table in the back yard, stirring our memories and watching them melt into another season.

We come together to remind each other of who we are individually and who we are as connected feminine energy. With a lineage that leads us to awakening our ancestors—stretching back to ancient ties, threading into all of us. Blood of our ancestors coursing through our veins, coursing into stories, and those stories circling back to us. The air becomes thick with their presence, and in this way we form a sacred circle of ceremony. We tell stories to remember, to make sense of our lives, to pass the information on from one generation to the next. We hold each other up.

Together, we remember who we are.

These women have the compassionate eyes of survivors. They allow me to look into the bottomless losses that connect with my more recent one. Judy's husband died young, like Jim, leaving her with three small children. Now in remission from her second bout of cancer, she smiles at me, showing me she has not only survived, but has transcended. Is it possible she is more beautiful now? Laura, whose 12-year-old daughter Tess is battling cancer, is telling a story while bent over laughing. Jennee, who almost died from a pregnancy, and before that gave birth to a baby angel who died an hour after being born. Great Aunt Olga, the last of nine children, guardian of generations of family secrets, survivor of many losses in her long lifetime. I see all of these women's beauty and the radiance that comes from transcending loss.

With my tribe of angels, I understand our connection with the beyond and the presence of heaven here on earth. We are being shaped by loss, all of us, and they love me with the compassion only survivors can offer. No longer only survivors, they are now victors. Their triumphant eyes tell me, "We're here to show you how strong you are." When I look into their eyes I see constellations and galaxies and ancient wisdom orbiting in them. I see unexpected gifts of loss: growth, gratitude, resilience, compassion, wisdom, and expanding hearts knowing how to love hugely.

Now my angel wings, still wounded, respond to the angel wings on the backs of these women who know me so well, and the memory of the unfolding of wings comes to my skin through them. My wings began to flutter in recognition, testing the breeze. A lightness I haven't felt since before Jim died runs down my neck, into my back, and I feel my heart opening.

Remember who you are.

We uncork more bottles and move on to cheaper bottles of wine. More stories, more laughter followed by tears. I tell them about the woman in California who had held me, who told me I would emerge from the trauma of Jim's death transformed from the experience, but strong and beautiful, like a butterfly. I tell them I will emerge, infused by the strength of our circle. I tell them I'm not quite there yet, but I can feel myself getting closer. I tell them how grateful I am, a word I thought would be erased forever from my vocabulary when Jim died.

And in this moment of sharing, in this sacred circle of loss and transformation, of resilience and expanding hearts, of gratitude for what is, we decide to call ourselves *The Butterfly Clan.*

We begin pounding the picnic table, drumming it with our hands, still laughing, causing the wine glasses to make music when glass touches glass. But on the fringe of that laughter is something mysterious as we pound the sound to bring in our ancestors. It becomes a ceremony as we call out to Big Mama and to her mama and further and further back, reaching to our Celtic ancestors, crossing the bridge between heaven and earth, calling to infinity and eternal spiritual love, all represented by the Celtic Cross ring wrapped around Jennee's finger. The pounding of fists on the table—a universal language while the fluttering of a million butterfly wings hover in the air, wings against wings against wings, speaking to the deeper connection of us all.

Remember who you are.

In our hearts we are always connected, but we

want something, a marker, something visible and tangible, something we can see because we can't see our own wings, we can only feel them. Someone suggests we get tattoos. We are not women who get tattoos.

Great Aunt Olga, former beauty queen, her beauty softened by her later years, is now peering out at us through a kitchen window while washing dishes. She yells, "Y'all can't get tattoos, it's not legal in Oklahoma!"

We go home, we leave our circle, but the circle doesn't leave us. We become women who get tattoos.

I am first. I go to a studio on St. Marks Place, one frequented by famous musicians and runway models. My friend Kendra goes with me to hold my hand. The tattoo artist's arms are so covered in symbols you can't see the color of natural skin—snakes and dragons and mermaids traveling down his arm. I show him the size of the butterfly I want on my skin. He shakes his head and says no. The size of the wings can't be that small, he insists. In the end I allow his artistic vision to burn into my skin, knowing that like the woman in California, he sees something in me that I haven't seen yet. He knows I will grow into the wings he chooses for me. Colorful, beautiful and vibrant. Ready to take me to some place new.

Each of us, one by one, brand our skin with butter-flies—on arms, shoulders, hips, and backs. Calling each other, showing the longitude and latitude of the burning on our bodies and the beauty continues to emerge from the pain.

I know this weekend will live inside all of us. Judy will lose her battle with cancer, and so will Tess, but I don't know that yet. Their wings will take them into the most sacred ancestral space we call in that weekend. Strong women. Strong angels. Easter weekend becomes a time of resurrection, of me moving beyond survivor and taking my place in the circle.

I emerge from the chrysalis slowly, hopeful for my future.

I remember who I am.

Gifts of Loss

People often talk about the gifts they have gained from loss and adversity. I know that many of the qualities I developed from a difficult childhood are qualities that helped me to succeed in my career: I am responsible, hard working, conscientious, loyal. I would never have thought of them as "gifts" until the perspective I gained after Jim died allowed me to see loss through a different lens.

I'd read here and there about people overcoming huge obstacles and calling them gifts, but never really "got it" until a few years after Jim's death. By then, I was hyper alert to anything I heard or read about how other people coped with the death of a loved one. At first, if anyone had told me there would be gifts that would follow I would not have believed them.

Maybe you have your own story of the gifts of loss. Or maybe you're still in the thick fog of grief and cannot imagine any gift ever coming from what you are now experiencing.

And that's okay. It is my hope that my story of healing gives you the faith that one day you'll feel better.

Gifts of growth. Gratitude. Compassion. Wisdom. An expanding heart. Resilience. An ability and desire to help others through similar experiences. An awareness of how the smallest gestures of kindness can hugely impact a life. Learning how to love hugely. Telling everyone you love that you love them. That you are grateful for them. Learning that love is always and forever. Love lives on in your heart. It does not die.

Just by being you, showing someone who is newly bereaved that you've survived—this is a gift because it gives that person the hope that they, too, will be able to survive.

for you

I'm grateful for my angels here on earth and on the other side. Some are people I've only met once (like the woman at the California retreat) and yet have had a profound impact on my life. Someone's kindness or what may seem like a small gesture on their part can change the course of a life. You can be an angel to someone without even knowing it. Often, when we've been through a life-altering loss, the compassion and empathy we gain translates into wanting to do something meaningful for others—a gift.

Look for the angels in your life. Call on them when you need them. Let your tribe embrace you and show you the way.

Often, great strength can be found in the stories of previous generations—what they had to overcome so that you can be here today.

Is there someone in your family who can share stories of how they've overcome tragedy?

Heavy
by Mary Oliver

That time
I thought I could not
go any closer to grief
without dying

I went closer,
and I did not die.
Surely God
had His hand in this,

as well as friends.
Still I was bent,
and my laughter,
as the poet said,

was nowhere to be found.
Then said my friend Daniel
(brave even among lions),
"It is not the weight you carry

but how you carry it—
books, bricks, grief—
it's all in the way
you embrace it, balance it, carry it

when you cannot, and would not,
put it down."
So I went practicing.
Have you noticed?

Have you heard
the laughter
that comes, now and again,
out of my startled mouth?

How I linger
to admire, admire, admire
the things of this world
that are kind, and maybe

also troubled—
roses in the wind,
The sea geese on the steep waves,
a love
to which there is no reply?

~ 13 ~

Ready to Dance Again

Attractive men across bars, across desks, at cocktail parties in the sky, in rooms crowded with tailored suits and black dresses and high heels and lipstick and laughter while the softly glowing lights of shimmering New York City nights illuminate seductive smiles. Trays of canapés and champagne mingle with music and merriment, and an aura of yes surrounds me.

I am still in a place of in between, no longer in my old life but not yet steady in the new one. But I know the time has come to step out of the shadows. I can feel the sun on my face and no longer associate it with pain. I wake early for work and appreciate the deep pinks and purples of sunrise as a crescent slice of sun appears shining up from the edges of the eastern horizon. I am this crescent sun. I have emerged from the chrysalis grateful, knowing I've survived something that seemed insurmountable two and half years earlier.

I attend parties and dinners and events and I begin to look at men again—to flirt back, to choose clothing that clings to my body differently, clothing that drapes and whispers. I was always around men in my profession but they moved past me like soldiers in my battle with grief and as part of the business world. But as my desire wakes up, I begin to test my wings and my smile toward men changes. I smile back in a quiet acceptance of their invitations. I am ready to join the dance again and the banter becomes more personal and playful.

I change my low-heeled pumps to strappy stilettos that lift my calves, and I wear sleek black dresses that hug my body and show me in the mirror the woman I am becoming. Shoes not made for walking, dresses not made for the business world. At work, I still wear the uniform of a suit and buttoned-up silk blouses, but at night a different me is showing up when it's not a business event.

If Jim were alive and saw me dressed in this way he would have said, "Honey, we're going to be late for dinner." And I don't want to be with anyone but Jim, but I also no longer want to be alone. I want someone who sees all of me, the way Jim did. I know no one will ever be like Jim was for me—I was a twenty-five-year-old girl when we met, but I am a woman now.

A woman who isn't looking for love yet, but a woman ready to be touched, a woman reawakening. I want mischievous eyes and dark, long hair curling over ears with charm and laughter and sexy smiles. My body switch has turned to "on" after being dormant for so long. My skin craves touch.

And then I see him at a party, from across the room—a man who works with my close friend Vin. His long dark lashes outline eyes of amusement, his full lips bloom into a smile. I feel it in the warmth spreading across my chest, and at the sight of his lips, mine part. His white teeth contrast with his tanned skin, which is covered by an expensive suit outlining a muscular body, and my toes curl in my shoes.

I say yes to him with my smile. Yes to another glass of champagne as he crosses the room. I hear my voice laughing at his jokes, I feel my body lean toward his body as the room gets louder and louder and we get closer and closer to hear each other. We are listening with our skin now. I can feel his body, his breath, as if his body is brushing against mine, but no, we haven't touched.

He is about to ask if I want to leave the party and get a drink somewhere else and I know I will say yes. I can feel the invitation in the air between us, when my friend Vin appears and speaks something in his ear and then takes my arm, and makes excuses as he leads me away. When we are far enough away, Vin tells me to watch out for him, tells me he is a player. Vin told him to stay away from me. Vin and his wife were good friends with Jim and I and they've been there for me since he died.

I am annoyed, but I know Vin knows how vulnerable I am; I'm not ready for the kind of guy who might further damage my fragile heart. At least not yet.

A few weeks later, after the almost seduction, I am set up on a blind date by a married girlfriend who gushes about all the wonderful qualities of this man— qualities that didn't seem to show up anywhere during our first and only date. The only thing we have in common is the woman who fixed us up. His smile is guarded, not laugh-filled, and he doesn't have mischievous eyes. Even worse, he is aggressive and unkind with the wait staff at my favorite Italian restaurant. I am embarrassed by his dismissive behavior and I can't wait to go home.

Once I'm home, I throw off my shoes and in a fit of fury begin to cry. My tears turn to sobs as the grief spiral takes me down and I land on the floor, still in my dress. I rage like I did the first few months after Jim died. Raging at God, the universe, and at Jim. *Why did you leave me, Jim? I don't want to do this!* What was missing in this man made me crave the qualities of Jim all over again—his kindness toward me and everyone we came into contact with. I imagine the future: going on dates and having my hard-earned hope be slowly squeezed out of me in these dinners with men who weren't Jim or anything like him. Who would ever meet my expectations?

Vin and his wife Teresa call to see how the date went and talk with me through my emotional spiral. I cry and they listen. Eventually, I exhaust myself with emotion and fall asleep. Reminding myself as I drift off that Jim wants me to be happy and I want to be happy too.

By the next morning, when Vin and Teresa call to check on me, I have calmed down. It was only a date, but it was a big first step for me. Now we all laugh as I tell them more details of the dismal date. The laughter is healing. The evening feels like a baptism into the new life of men and dating. I am just beginning and the barometer is now low. Once I get past this first disappointment, the door to having fun swings wide open, and I am standing in it, ready and waiting.

And then finally: him. We talk on the phone every day for months before we eventually meet in person at a business event. He seems nice, but I feel little chemistry and no sparks. Still, I say yes when he asks me out, because I think he is nice, and why not? It will be good practice.

But when he picks me up, he is wearing jeans and a close-fitting shirt unbuttoned all the way to sexy. Looking very different from the man who wore the suit the week before, his professional veneer hanging in his closet at home. Now I see the amusement in his eyes and the playfulness in his smile, and when I open the door I feel he sees all of me. With a confidence that speaks to the waking woman in me, he takes my hand. Small explosions of desire take me by surprise.

In the crowded restaurant we are alone in our own universe, barely eating, neither one of us able to stop smiling as our eyes meet from across the table. We both know, without a word. With the touch of hand. He sees me and he gets me. He knows what I need, and my skin begins to burn in anticipation and it feels good. So good to be desired and to desire like this. To know touch is on the way.

This isn't about falling in love. I am falling in lust. Later, when his mouth presses into mine, I know he is the perfect first guy.

Stepping Out of the Shaddows

If you've lost a lover, partner or spouse, there are many complicated feelings that arise when you begin to date and become intimate with someone again. For some people, it's soon and that's okay, especially if their loved one died after a long illness. It doesn't mean they've healed or have "gotten over" their loss. It's their way of feeling alive again and it's totally fine. Or it may be a year, or two, or longer, and that's okay, too. Some people feel guilty, like they're cheating on their loved one, or not honoring their memory. Someone might say to you, "so soon?" OR "isn't it time?" No one can tell you how it's supposed to be. You'll know when the time is right for you.

About a year or so after Jim died several people asked when I was going to be ready to date again. It was really easy to slip into feeling that I wasn't living up to a societal rulebook of grief. I wasn't ready, but I thought, should I be ready? Is something wrong that I'm not? Am I ever going to be ready?

Stepping out of the shadows felt really good after more than two years of not being ready. I had taken the time I needed to cocoon and heal. I missed Jim, still cried easily and often, visited his grave regularly, and pulled out the blue box of memories. I took the anniversary of his death off work for several years. When I had grief spirals like I did the night of that first date, I found I began to recover or bounce back more quickly as time went by. The stretches between the dark days became longer and longer as my resilience grew.

When I turned forty, I had a party to celebrate that I had not only survived, but was thriving, happy, and grateful. I had learned how to live again. Fully. I still grieved, but it was a pain I'd learned how to live with. I invited everyone who had been there for me. It was wonderful. When I looked around the room at all these very special people I felt truly blessed. Jim smiled with us.

It was what he would want for me. And soon enough, I was able to stop reminding myself of this—as though I had *to give myself permission to enjoy and savor life again. Not long after my fortieth birthday, I fell in love.*

for you

Cathy, a client of mine, met someone she was very attracted to a few months after her husband died of cancer. Although she knew her late husband wanted her to be happy, she wondered if it was "too soon." In our sessions, she was able to talk freely about the myriad emotions she was experiencing: the excitement she felt with this new man, the hope it gave her for the future, the guilt she felt for thinking it was too soon, the apprehension in wondering how it would feel to be with another man after fifteen years of only being with her husband, the anger she felt because her husband had died, and the grief she was still feeling—she missed her husband very much.

Cathy learned she had room for both her grief and for this new relationship. She was ready.

When you're ready, you'll know it. There is no timetable. Some people struggle with feelings of guilt and some don't. Don't let the "shoulds" decide for you. Do what feels right for you.

When you have an episode of overwhelming grief even years later, just know this is natural. As we know, grief is not linear; even years later you might feel like you've gone back to what it felt like in the beginning. Having my therapist to help me navigate the ups and downs and what felt like going backwards was crucial to my healing. You don't have to do it alone—if it's an option, find a qualified professional. If not, ask someone you trust who can help by listening and supporting you.

Through the night with a light from above

— *Irving Berlin*

~ 14 ~

Turning Point

My boyfriend has called from a plane at the airport just to say good morning and goodbye as he left for a two-day business trip. I am back into the world of relationship and routine. I am on my second cup of coffee in my midtown office, getting ready for a hectic day as the senior securities trader for a money management firm.

I have a television on as I do every day to keep up with the news of the stock market, sound muted so I can focus on trades for the day ahead. I'm absorbed in work, reading research notes and shuffling through paper, when my phone rings and changes everything. My friend from Jersey City asks me if I saw what happened, asks if my television is on. There is something unsteady about his voice that makes me not want to look at my television screen.

But I do look up, as the whole world looks up with me. My friend says something I can't comprehend at first—that a plane flew into the World Trade Center. He could see it from his office overlooking the Hudson River.

September 11th started as a beautiful day, with a cloudless blue sky and crisp air that hinted of autumn— but in a moment, everything changes.

Watching the television, my body goes weightless, like my skin will dissolve into my swivel chair. I think of my boyfriend. Is he safe? Yes, I know he is, he called again when his plane landed. The next hour and forty-five minutes are a blur of panicked phone calls and scenes of war, my co-workers buzzing around my office like bees in a hive on their phones, grabbing slices of information: which floor was hit, which floors were above the floor that was hit. We wait, frozen, feeling the heartbeat of the whole world and watch the day unfold, helpless.

The South Tower collapses at 9:59 a.m. and the North Tower at 10:28 a.m. I feel an implosion, my bones melting as we watch the twin pillars of New York collapse and disintegrate on our televisions, blocks downtown from us. It's hard to imagine the majestic towers as real; they seem to topple like small toys because they are miniature on my screen, like a movie with fire and smoke. Watching the big on the small of my screen, I say a prayer of denial, that this violation of humanity cannot be real. But the screams I hear from my own mouth, in my office, the screams I hear from across continents and oceans assure me this is real. This is real.

And the whole world changes again, only this time not just for me but for everyone.

People pour into the street, out of tall buildings that now feel unsafe to be inside. Confusion and shock in eyes with heads back and necks exposed, everyone looking up, peering up at a still perfect blue sky, surreal now after seeing the collapse minutes before. I look downtown and see the opaque black cloud begin to eclipse the blue.

We walk into the thickness of a world changing before us, walking in shock, people on cell phones, frantic sirens coming from every direction, not knowing what is next, hearing details in fragments of conversation. Nobody knowing how to get home, where their loved ones are, racing to pick up children from schools, everyone pouring into the streets of New York in a mixture of sound and silence, all of us reaching out to each other, holding each other up.

I overhear snippets of sentences with the hushed tone of stunned disbelief: *It will be all right, no I haven't heard, I hear the ferry is running, the subways are shut down, a plane crashed in Pennsylvania...* This mixed with the silence of shock. In the between moments we pray for all the people, but especially those that worked on the highest floors—were any able to escape before the collapse?

Black fighter jets circle low in the sky, the sound of their engines a constant reminder that something is very wrong. Those of us able to go home do so, bringing friends and co-workers with us who are stranded in the city. A woman is crying, asking if we're going to die, *do the planes mean chemical warfare?* I can't see her through the mass of people, I can only hear her panic and thoughts. We are a sea of sickened souls moving through the concrete city as if through swampland. Slow, slow, sirens screaming like our throats want to scream, the sirens screaming for all of us, all of us disoriented, circling toward home or at least the temporary shelter of friends' homes.

My apartment becomes one of those shelters.

The city is on lockdown. We watch images on the news with the rest of the world, all of our eyes the same eyes— we want to forget the images the minute we see them. We cannot look and we cannot look away, absorbing all the suffering and distributing it among all of us. We will never forget, along with the rest of the world. It was happening to our friends, our loved ones, our colleagues, in our city. Inside those buildings are fathers, mothers, wives, husbands, children, and friends.

We look into the dark debris on my television with hands over our mouths. So many people I know and love inside those buildings. So many of my colleagues in our tight-knit financial community.

We wait for injured people to be carried out of the destruction and emerge from the darkness. We watch. We sit vigil. We think by giving our full attention we can will every soul to come back to us.

Phones are working intermittently and hours go by. Nobody walks out of the debris. Nobody is carried out of the darkness. By nighttime, the entire world realizes that no matter how long we sit vigil, no one is going to emerge. It is many days before we give up hope, and until the funerals begin, hope lingers.

The funerals and memorials continue for months—this is how I spend my weekends. I visit the homes of the grieving and find I am able to hold space for the grief with them. I am able to look into the eyes of the widows. In witnessing their trauma, I understand the gift of being with Jim when he died, I have the gift of knowing Jim did not die in fear or pain. And until this moment, until the funerals and the hundreds of grieving eyes of other widows, I did not understand this as a gift.

I find I can hold gazes in a way very few could hold mine when I was a new widow, connecting through the empathy of a shared experience of loss, and the human need for compassion and love. I can bear their hearts hurting when they can't bear it.

Many of the grieving know my husband died suddenly and see me as a thread of hope. They tell me, because I am still here, a survivor, this means they might survive, too. Helping others helps me get through this dark time and offers me the gift of finding greater purpose and meaning in my own life. This gift is nurtured by the seeds of my own sorrow, and with this gift, I am able to give to others. September 11th begins to show me how.

Seeds of Sorrow Bloom

September 11th shows us the power of what happens when we come together in a shared experience of grief, humanity, and love. Together, we shoulder grief and we carry it together—this is how we get through it. We are all connected and in times like this we remember.

It was a major turning point in my life, as it was for many. My ability to hold grief for others planted the seeds of changing the direction of my life. My understanding of my past was transformed and reaffirmed that day even though it wasn't clear to me until much later. After deep contemplation and reflection, I eventually left the financial world to become a therapist so I could help others like my therapist helped me. This decision transformed my life and in doing so helped me to help others transform theirs. I like to think of it as a legacy from Jim.

for you

In helping others, even when in the midst of our own grief, we can help ourselves. By doing something for someone else, in helping someone in the same way others helped me, I feel my best. For me, this is what living a life with meaning is about—effecting change in the world, in our own way, for the good of ourselves and of others. As so beautifully expressed by St. Francis of Assisi: it is in giving that we receive.

EXPANDING INTO THE MYSTERY

Really important meetings are planned by the souls
long before the bodies see each other.

— *Paulo Coelho*

~ 15 ~

I Didn't Want To Know

The first time was the July before Jim died. He called me at work and said, "I should be dead." My chest constricted with the truth in his words because Jim wasn't the kind of man who called and said such things. It was a Friday morning, and he was driving to Martha's Vineyard without me. I asked him what happened, what was wrong, and my body began to mirror his shaking voice. While driving on I-95 a tractor-trailer lost a wheel, and the trailer swerved in front of him, missing him by a small measure, less than the width of his hand.

Jim told me he was shaking all over, his whole body, repeating that he should be dead. I shook along with him, his brush with death flowing through the phone.

That day, with me at the office, and Jim on his way to our favorite vacation spot without me, I didn't recognize this almost accident as the first sign. I would have rushed to join Jim and not wasted five days working during a busy trading time that seemed so important then but in retrospect seems meaningless. If I'd seen it as the first sign of what was to come, I would not have stayed at my desk. Missing the first five days of our last vacation together is still one of my biggest regrets.

My body shivered in a kind of realization, and I felt light-headed with thoughts of what would have happened if he had crashed. *I couldn't bear it. I couldn't live if he died.* I tried to shake the dark thoughts off of me and focus on comforting him. I pushed those thoughts away like a fire extinguisher puts out a flame before it erupts into a blaze. Death brushed him by inches and he survived. That was all that mattered and I denied the apprehension, though I felt weak for hours after.

The second time was late September, when Jim and I were at an intersection near our home in Long Island, waiting for the light to turn green. It was an ordinary fall day and he was talking about work, or his children, or something he read in a magazine, and I glanced at him as he talked, me in the passenger seat and his hands on the steering wheel, the face I loved still tanned from the summer sun. An uninvited thought pierced through the ordinary. *What if something happened to him?* And a chill spread through my body, the same chill that had entered when I answered the phone in July.

The possibility of my life without Jim was incomprehensible to me, and yet something seemed to be calling me to comprehend it. I didn't want to—*I couldn't bear it*—and I put my cold hand on Jim's warm thigh to push the thought away.

And the third time was mid-October in our bedroom. The sun's light was muted through the shaded bedroom windows, where most mornings I moved slowly from the unconscious dream state of sleep where all things can be known, to the conscious world of our life together. Another cold sensation spread through my body, and I awoke swiftly and sharply. I could hear my own heartbeat in the rhythm of our bed, with Jim sleeping peacefully beside me. I also heard a message: I was not going to have a baby.

We had been trying for almost a year, making love during ovulation, phone calls from work to say, *hurry home, it's time,* weekend lovemaking that went on from Friday night through Sunday evening. Inviting our love to create more love—the dream we had of bringing our child into the world.

That morning knowledge we were not going to have a baby was delivered to me from a place more powerful than both of us. A blanket of dread pulled itself up to my chin and I began to silently cry the tears of an almost mother. I didn't want to wake him with my sorrow. But he knew me, he felt me, it was how we were together, and soon his arms were wrapped around me as he asked what could be wrong. And I told him, while he wiped my tears and stroked my cold skin and kissed my eyes. He reassured me, of course we would have a child, of course we would make a new life together.

I let his words soothe me, as he cradled me in his arms like a lullaby. Because I wanted to believe him and not believe the dread. I wasn't wired to listen to dire messages and alarming thoughts. I was wired to trust Jim and our love. With his words and strong arms wrapped around me I was able to push the cold away. I let him soothe me back to sleep to the innocence of us, believing that everything was going to be okay.

Two weeks later, when the sun had yet to outline the borders of our bedroom shades, Jim woke up for the last time.

I am thankful for the gifts of all these moments with Jim, even those moments that tried to prepare us for what was to come. That morning, something in both of us knew what was happening was much bigger than a simple case of heartburn. We looked into each others eyes, said our I-love-yous, and for a brief moment, that moment before everything changed, we stood in the knowing of what was to follow. We stared at fate together.

Debbie Augenthaler

Premonitions

We all use denial as a way to avoid dealing with painful and/or scary feelings, thoughts, and emotions. Denial is a natural defense, a human response to daily life. If we live our lives always fearing the worst it would be hard to function in a healthy way. Often, people experience premonitions and don't fully realize they are premonitions until later. There are hundreds of stories about premonitions experienced by people before 9/11.

Many people have one or more premonitions before a loved one dies, especially with sudden death. Often, these moments, thoughts, and feelings of dread that we may have cast aside come flooding back and we wonder why we didn't listen, why we didn't pay attention. They were pushed away because it's unimaginable something so terrible could happen.

Intersections are incredible metaphors for change, although I didn't know it at the time. I'd forgotten the premonitions because they were so painful to imagine. After Jim died, I remembered these three incidents. And then I couldn't stop remembering, wondering if there was anything I could have done to save Jim's life. Some people take comfort in believing premonitions are tied to destiny and nothing could have been done to change the lamentable outcome.

for you

You may have experienced your own premonitions, and perhaps, like me, pushed them away. It helps to talk about this, especially if you have a running commentary going through your mind like I did. The "why didn't I do this or that" kind of inner talk that can make your grieving even more painful than it already is. Or you may not have had any premonitions, and that's okay, too. Remember: there is nothing we can do to change someone else's destiny, no matter how desperately we wish we could.

Hear from the heart wordless mysteries!
Understand what cannot be understood!
In man's stone-dark heart there burns a fire
That burns all veils to their root and foundation.
When the veils are burned away,
the heart will understand completely
Ancient Love will unfold ever-fresh forms
In the heart of the Spirit, in the core of the heart.

— *Rumi (translated by Andrew Harvey)*

~ 16 ~

Tell Everyone

Before Jim entered my life I had my Aunt Jennee—she was the one always on the other end of the phone ready to give me advice and share my joy and my sorrow. When I was a child I felt glued to the side of her body, entranced by her every movement as she moved gracefully through adolescence, her long, auburn hair in big hot curlers, applying makeup, smiling as she applied lipstick to my seven-year-old mouth, and sharing with me all the things a girl needs to know before going on a date.

I lived with Jennee and my grandparents when my father was in the fields of war on the other side of the world, and she was there for me when my father returned a stranger to our small Alabama town, Jennee shielding me from his dark, watchful eyes.

I watched her glide through her bedroom and choose dresses for dates, teaching me everything I needed to know about life: how to hold my tummy in when I was older, how to paint fingernails, how to play "Chopsticks" on the piano, and other things my 16-year-old aunt deemed important for me to know. Everyone thought we were sisters, and I followed her around like a little sister, smelling the scent of her drugstore perfume on my skin long after she disappeared into the car of a local boy.

***

And now, here I am delayed in the Chicago airport in the middle of a blizzard, on the telephone, and my cousin has called me to tell me Jennee is dying—Jennee, who was healthy just this morning when I left Tulsa after a family celebration. Jennee, who was my maid of honor when I married Jim, who was by my side when I buried him, and who held my sorrow in the aftermath of 9/11. Here at O'Hare, looking out the window, I am seven years old again, glued to her side and facing the possibility that she will die. I want to help her as she has helped me all these years, but I'm staring out the window watching a million snowflakes stick to the runway, the airplanes lined up like birds with broken wings.

In a hospital in Tulsa, her throat is closing and her lungs are burning and she is drowning in a vast sea of air that can't push past the closures in her body. Jennee, who is all the goodness in the world, can no longer breathe and is turning blue, and I love her and I feel her pain, and I call on God, on the Universe, on Divine Love with the noise of an overburdened airport in the background. I chant a prayer of intention to keep her here: *save her, save her, save her.*

I don't know that she is returning home at this moment, to the place we are all from. I don't know that at this moment her pain has disappeared and a gentle wave of energy is holding her and floating her out of the hospital room.

I don't know she is already in a new place and my voice asking to save her is actually calling for her return. She is moving through time and space, through other lifetimes, the ancient of all of it surrounding her with the most beautiful love and peace she has ever felt.

Save her, save her, save her.

And Jennee suddenly knows, in the softness of this bliss, of being surrounded by everyone she's ever loved, that she is dying, that she has left her body. I'm not ready to die, she thinks, and there is my chant, my prayer, calling her back to us: *save her, save her, save her.*

In the hospital, Jennee inhales sharply, fighting to draw back in her life, as the doctor injects prednisone into her veins, and oxygen feeds her starving lungs.

A few hours later we are able to speak on the phone. I am still in the airport, trying to find my way back to her.

"Debbie," she says, "Tell everyone."

Her voice is a tired, hoarse whisper, and my wet face soaks the phone in gratitude that I get to hear her speak to me again.

"Tell everyone how beautiful it is. Divine peace and love are waiting for us on the other side. It's always there, and everyone needs to know."

I ask her if Jim was there too. If I couldn't glimpse him, then maybe she could bring a sign of him back to me.

"Oh, Deb, it wasn't like that. But of course he was there, along with everything and everyone that ever was and ever will be."

Holding the phone, sitting at the airport, I want to experience death with Jennee, even for a moment, just to be near Jim in that way again. And then, with the heat running through the vents in the overheated airport, I feel a cool breeze against my neck. I know Jim is telling me I don't need to taste death to feel him.

His love is with me always. And so is the Divine Love that connects us all.

Tell everyone.

Infinite Love

Most of us have heard of near death experiences (NDEs), but not many of us have had one. The numerous bestselling books on the subject prove the strong interest in wanting to know what happens when we die. All around the world, people have come back from an NDE with similar stories of peace, love, and light. Clearly, the Divine wants us to know the transition is beautiful and that we are met with the love we are always connected to. I share Jennee's story because it is comforting and because of the message she came back with to tell everyone. I could hear the truth in her voice and the incredible comfort she felt.

We are separated from other dimensions by the veils of being human, but there are times when the veil is thinner, allowing us to see the truth that spirit lives on and that we are all connected by infinite Divine Love. It is in each and every one of us.

for you

You might find it comforting to read of others' near death experiences—to think of your loved one being met with infinite love and peace as he or she transitioned from this life. It's also comforting for us to know that when our time comes, we will be met with peace and surrounded by infinite love.

There are many bestselling books about NDEs. *Proof of Heaven* by Eben Alexander, a neurosurgeon, and *Dying to Be Me* by Anita Moorjani, are two of my favorites.

Love, the new moon, grows slowly, stage by stage;
We should progress like that, deliberately, with patience.
I hear the new moon whispering, "Impatient fool!"
It is only step by step you climb to the roof.

— Rumi (translated by Andrew Harvey)

~ 17 ~

Moon - Light

My love for the moon began when I was seven, as my dad and I nestled into the damp grass of dark while he pointed to the stars and constellations and told me stories of Zeus and Orion and the Seven Sisters. Stories of the Greek gods and far away galaxies and mysteries held in the twinkling sky. Mesmerized by the moon, I saw a wink of recognition. She beckoned, inviting my young mind to open up to possibilities far beyond the small square of neatly mown grass in front of our house.

The moon has helped me through many transitions in my life, but especially through all the ones of losing Jim—not realizing she's been preparing me for loss all along, as her quiet face, still beckoning, moves an inch and a half further away from the earth each year. She has been my guide, helping me move forward, and whenever I am lost, even on a cloudy night when I can't see her enthralling luminescence, I know she is there: as a full moon, a new moon, a crescent, or a quarter. Even if I can't see all of her, knowing she is there is enough. Constant, no matter where I am.

Through this long passage of losing Jim, which after twenty years still continues, the moon has mirrored my emotions. Sometimes joyful, like the full moon, feeling balanced, brilliant and whole, sure of my place in the world. And other times, feeling like the thin sliver of crescent moon, light diminished, withdrawing into myself. Yet my light has always been there, even when I couldn't see it.

When I have forgotten who I am, when I am not sure of where I am going, when I am cloaked in darkness, all I needed is a glimpse of my true self, and I often find that glimpse mirrored in her face. Wink. Then I begin again, and rediscover, once more, the resiliency and strength to grow. The moon has mirrored every transition that followed grief, all the times I needed to cocoon, to heal, and to transform.

Walking the streets of New York to go to my job, and home, and out to dinner, she has always been there, above the skyscrapers, in between buildings, or tucked behind them on a horizon line I couldn't see, spreading her magic light on everything. I may look like the same Debbie to everyone else, but I am never the same as the last moon. I change with her, moving further from my crushing grief a little at a time, just as she has been moving slowly away from earth since she was formed.

Does the moon know where she is going? Do I know where I am going? I am beginning to learn the destination is not as important as the cycle of life, and while beginnings always have an end, the very nature of endings are new beginnings. I often start with the lunar cycle all over again, through all the phases—including the next new beginning. The awareness of the cycle, the tides that go in and out and the slow rotation of the earth, is like a perfect cosmic dance.

And yet, the ever-changing moon is an illusion because all of her is always there, even when you can't see it. Even in the darkest times, when we feel hopeless, a spark of soul essence is waiting patiently for the shadow to pass so our light can grow stronger, and be full and whole and brilliant again.

The moon is there for all of us. And she illuminates not just ourselves but the light that is in us, streaming between us, reminding us how deeply connected we are to each other—a connection that never ends.

Just as one candle lights another
and can light thousands of other candles,
so one heart illuminates another heart
and can illuminate thousands of other hearts.

— *Leo Tolstoy*

Healing Light

We all have changes, transitions, and transformation in our lives. Endings and beginnings are a lifelong journey and process. We all have times of sorrow, sadness, hope, joy and growth, shedding old ways and growing into new ways of being.

Loss of any kind can bring great gifts, to yourself and to others. There is no way for us to know this at the beginning of grief. If someone had told me this in the first few months after Jim died, I might have slapped them and said, "How can you say that? How, in any way, can this ever be seen as a gift?" It takes time, and it certainly doesn't mean the loss is the gift. It's what comes after the loss. It's what we learn in the process of grieving, who we become afterwards.

We have all heard people say, "If THAT terrible event hadn't happened, then I wouldn't have had the chance for THIS meaningful opportunity." Everything from starting charities, to parents who have lost children and gone to Washington to change legislation, to volunteering to help those in need, and so much more. Foundations have been started, books have been written, new love has formed. So much good coming out of so much pain. All of it shapes who we become.

If I had not gone through the losses I did, I wouldn't be who I am today.

If your loss one day will enable you to reach another and touch even ONE other person in a positive way in their time of need—loving them, supporting and encouraging them—whom might they help in return? One simple gesture of kindness and compassion can start a wave of healing light that ripples out and affects countless others.

In saving others we often save ourselves. By helping others to heal, we help heal ourselves. We begin to discover threads of meaning, however small, that can start to be woven into shaping a new life.

As you continue on your own healing journey, as you do the courageous, hard, exhausting work of grieving, healing, and growing, by just being who you are, you will help others through their own struggles. You can be a ray of hope. They'll think, "Well, look at her, look what she's been through, and she's still walking. Maybe that means I can survive, too."

for you

Go out and look at the moon. If it's a clear night, notice the whole moon and the shadow. Think of your whole self always being a part of you, even when you can't feel all of yourself, all of your brightness.

Watch the cycle of the moon as a meditation throughout the month. Look at the stars and the light and let them speak to you. What do you hear?

Why should I be out of mind because I am out of sight?
I am but waiting for you, for an interval,
somewhere very near

— *Henry Scott-Holland*

Welcome Home

by Debbie Augenthaler

His soul flew out the window.
Whatever I believed about the universe flew out too.
I didn't know it in that moment.
I didn't know anything for a while.
And that had to be.

My universe changed
inside and out.
A big bang event
birthing a new universe
for me.
A big bang event rippling out
with understanding,
like light years, taking a very long time.

All these years to know light surrounds me.
Light is in me.
A light I recognized,
like a long lost friend.

Oh there you are.
     I know you.
        I see you.
           I remember you.

I began to see its brilliance in the last few years.
In universe time
its journey to me smaller than a flicker of a thought.

His soul flew out the window.
A shimmering of stardust flying back
to the light from which it came.
A fireworks of star brilliance, star radiance, a soul star
burst.
Exploding and spinning back up
in a magnificent dance of whirling swirling light.

Soul star burst dancing back
to where all lights meet yet again.
Back to where our lights have met
again and again and again.
And in that moment
yet again.

His light connecting with mine
up where soul star bursts meet.
The touch of his light
telling mine
it was time to travel.
She cannot feel her light
as light embraced light.
Go to her, she needs you.

In record time for the universe
but light years for mortals
shimmering light travelled
and infused me with my soul star radiance.

Ah, yes,
> *I know you.*
>> *I see you.*
>>> *I remember you.*

For when our lights meet here
and when our lights meet there
and when our lights meet in between
it is known.

221

Debbie Augenthaler

Our lights are forever entwined
in a love embrace.

Along with everyone and everything
that ever was and ever will be.
The beautiful connection of light and love
we all are.

> *Oh there you are.*
> > *I know you.*
> > > *I see you.*
> > > > *I remember you.*

And now I feel this light,
mine and his and yours,
shining in me.
Light of love connecting
everyone and everything
that ever was and ever will be.

Reminding us of home.
Of our home. Of ancient homes.
Of ancient lives, of other lives, of other galaxies.

In the depths of the ocean
on the peaks of mountains
in the ground, in the clouds, in the wind
in the moon, in the stars.

Stars so far away
it cannot be measured.
Where soul star bursts dance back
to join together yet again.
All of them home.

Ah, yes,

    I know you.

        I see you.

            I remember you.

Really I am the soft stars that shine at night.
Do not stand at my grave and cry,
I am not there; I did not die.

— *Mary Elizabeth Frye*

~ 18 ~

Still Transforming

I often think of our "Harvest Moon" dance and the promise of always and forever love from Jim two weeks before he died. When I could see the moon with clear eyes again, I understood. The moon is always there, even when we can't see it, just like our connection to our loved ones. But we can sense it, we dream about it, we have signs, hints, and mysteries to show us.

What I didn't know for a good long while is that the past, the present, and my future was still hiding behind the stars, behind the moon. And then one night, as I slept in the parallel universe, the star that was holding my light, having itself slept a good long while, was nudged awake. Exploding awakening of star, star light, star knowledge, light expanding from the black hole energy lurking behind the experience of losing my husband. It was time for me to wake up. Wake up to the truth of the light. Wake up to the illusion of loss. And I did.

Life, loss, energy, expansion, everything is on a continuum of transformation. This is a law of science, of physics. The law of conservation states energy continues always. It can't be created or destroyed, it just transforms from one form to another. Our connection with everyone and everything that ever was and will be is always present. In this dimension we feel the dark nights of the soul. We feel loss and we grieve. This is our human experience. I still grieve Jim's loss and always will. Yet beyond the grieving is healing and hope and the knowledge we are always connected.

I know Jim still lives on in spirit and in me. Since his soul flew out the window in the early morning light, he's been with me always in my heart. Being seen by him, his nurturance, his love, his humor, lit a spark in the part of me afraid to love yet yearning for it. He taught me to trust in love, trust in him, and trust in myself. I am deeply grateful for the time we had together—it is the biggest gift of my life.

Loving him, losing him, grieving him—the entire experience of us expands my heart and my life in so many ways. Taking me to places and to doing things I would never have imagined or dreamed of as a young girl. Giving me the gift of being able to be with others in their grief, with deep compassion, with heart connection, holding space and holding gazes of eyes glazed with grief and locked with shock. It is a privilege and an honor to share this space.

My heart is still expanding, allowing me to leave pieces of him and our love in the hearts of others. Leading me to hold my head up, open up my arms and my heart, embrace the world, embrace this life, this day, this hour, this moment, this.

A Wish for You

I share my journey of grief, healing, and spiritual transformation to help hold and comfort you on yours. Twenty years ago I thought I'd never feel joy again. Yet I do. It is my joy and honor to share my experience and what I've learned with you. It is my wish this book will offer you hope and guide you through the labyrinth of loss to the other side of grief, when you are transformed by the gifts of loss.

Love lives always in our hearts,
and we are all connected.

Appendix:

How To Help

For Grievers & For Those Who Want To Help

The friend who can be silent with us
in a moment of despair or confusion,
who can stay with us in an hour of grief and bereavement,
who can tolerate not knowing...
not healing, not curing...
that is a friend who cares.

— *Henri Nouwen*

Inappropriate Comments, Advice, and Awkward Situations

IF YOU ARE GRIEVING:

One of the most helpful pieces of advice I received came from a close friend. On the day Jim died, she said, "People will say things to you that you won't believe. Try not to let it bother you. It's because they don't know what to say." It was valuable to remember this during the long hours standing in the receiving line during the four separate wakes.

This advice is helpful to keep in mind as time goes on. People will still say things that leave you stunned, shocked, or hurt. One of my clients showed up at my office and her held-back tears overflowed as soon as she walked in. Her mother had died about four months before and one of her co-workers asked when she was going to be ready to move on. We all grieve in our own way, in our own time. Don't let anyone tell you how you should grieve.

IF SOMEONE YOU KNOW IS GRIEVING:

As I stood with Jim's family in the receiving line at one of the wakes, with his open casket nearby, an older woman said, "Oh, honey, you're young. You'll meet someone else and marry again." I could taste blood as I bit my lip to not scream. I know she meant well, but don't ever say that to someone as she's standing near her husband's casket two days after he's died. And if someone's child has died, don't say, "Thank God you still have other children."

A former work colleague, someone I had not seen for a few years, said, "Wow, you look great, I mean, even with all that's happening. When the dust settles, do you want to go for a drink?" In disbelief, with my face swollen and red from tears and the strain of standing up when all I wanted to do was collapse and crawl into a hole, I couldn't help myself. I said, "The dust will never settle." I couldn't look at him again and recoiled as he tried to embrace me.

If you don't know what to say, a simple "I'm sorry" is fine. Please don't feel the need to "fill in" or grasp for something to say unless it is genuinely sympathetic, compassionate, and supportive. Not knowing what to say and saying nothing more than "I'm sorry" or giving a hug of support is hugely preferable to awkward words that fluster both you and the griever.

Even The Small Things Count

IF YOU ARE GRIEVING:

Let people help you.

IF SOMEONE YOU KNOW IS GRIEVING:

If the loss is new, in the first few weeks, do more than ask, "What can I do?" Call on your way to the grocery store, asking if there is anything you can pick up. Make a meal and drop it off. Ask if there are any errands that need to be done. If someone has children, offer to take them for a day or an evening, to give someone private time to grieve.

If you see them on the street or in the store, walk up and let them know you care. You can say, "You are in my thoughts" or, "How are you doing today?" Every day is different. Some days are better than others. If they don't want to engage, they will let you know. Please respect that too and continue to try to offer support at another time. Just because a grieving person says "no" once doesn't mean they never want you to ask again.

The Importance of Support

IF YOU ARE GRIEVING:

Let people support you. And if you need time alone to feel your feelings, to wail, to rage, pound a pillow, whatever it is you need to do, do it. If you have children, ask someone to babysit. Or maybe you don't want to be alone, and that's fine too. Whatever feels right to you. And remember, this will change, from day to day, minute to minute, week to week.

IF SOMEONE YOU KNOW IS GRIEVING:

In the first few weeks and months, people called me every single night. Almost like a tag team of family and friends, just to check in and make sure I was all right. They would listen when I wanted to talk. I didn't always want to, but knowing people cared and were there for me meant so much.

Close friends would frequently stop by to check in and would understand if I didn't want to engage. I often wouldn't want to—so please understand this about people grieving. We want and need your love and support. But at times we may not be very responsive to your efforts.

So be there for us and let us know it—call, stop by, show you care, but understand that some of us need space to grieve privately. Yet knowing someone is there, waiting, with love and acceptance matters more than you know.

Notes and Cards

IF YOU ARE GRIEVING:

I received hundreds of letters and cards, some of them from people I didn't know but who knew Jim. They shared their memories of him: of the difference he made in their lives, kind gestures, kind words, or a funny story. I read each one, over and over. It meant so much and brought me comfort. It was wonderful to see how special others thought he was, too.

IF SOMEONE YOU KNOW IS GRIEVING:

Take the time to send that card or letter. It matters more than you can imagine. A sympathy card is fine, but if you have a special memory to share, that will be comforting and special. Some people don't send cards because they don't know what to say. Again, "I'm sorry" is meaningful and supportive.

It's Not About You, It's About Them

IF YOU ARE GRIEVING:

Do you feel the need to censor or suppress yourself because you're concerned how someone else may feel? Has someone avoided you or, because they don't know what to say, become uncomfortable if you talk about your loved one? When someone says something hurtful or inappropriate, try not to take it personally—it's about them, not you. It's about their own fear, their own discomfort, and not knowing what to say.

Surround yourself with those who will listen and hold the space with you. Who can be completely present with you while you talk about your loved one, about this new life you're living and how hard it is to navigate, about your fears, your new rituals, what help you still need, about anything and everything. Find people who give you the freedom to be just who you are and where you are at this very moment.

IF SOMEONE YOU KNOW IS GRIEVING:

As a psychotherapist, and as someone who's experienced loss, I can't tell you how many times I've been asked by people who want to help, "What do I say? What can I do?" I hope the following is helpful.

Grievers live in a world of Before and After, learning how to live with huge holes in their lives. There is no compass or map or how-to manual to help navigate the world of After. If you aren't sure what to say, a simple "I'm sorry" is fine. Acknowledging the loss is what's important. This is kind and supportive.

A gentle clasp of the hand, a hug, sharing a kind thought like, "I think of him often and miss him" is welcomed. Or, "You and your family are in my prayers." We want our loved ones to be remembered and missed and want to talk about the person we love, whose love is still alive, carried in our hearts. Whose energy is still all around us and always will be. We don't want to be concerned we might cause others discomfort because we still talk about the person we love. All the time. We want to know it's okay. Because it is!

Hold that space for us. Listen, even if we tell the same story over and over. At the very least, don't avert your eyes. Don't walk away. Don't treat us as if we're invisible.

Special Note:

I knew how important it was to Jim to be a donor, and it gave me some solace. I never asked the doctors what he donated. All I knew was, because he had died immediately, it couldn't be his heart or major organs. However, within a couple of months I started receiving letters in the mail from various organizations thanking him for being a donor and what was donated. They thought his family would like to know who and how he helped others after he died. Every time I opened the mailbox and opened a letter of gratitude, I'd feel a fresh punch to my stomach and cry. But then I'd read it again and take comfort in knowing how many people he helped because of his generosity. The letters were a mixed blessing.

If you're so inclined, become an organ donor. Let your loved ones know your wishes. It's a beautiful gift to someone whose life will be forever changed.

Here is the link to the National Organ Registry: www.organdonor.gov

About the Author:
Debbie Augenthaler, LMHC, NCC

Debbie is a writer and psychotherapist in New York City, where she has specialized in trauma, grief, and loss. Prior to becoming a therapist she had a successful career in the financial industry for more than twenty years.

She has a Master's Degree in Counseling for Mental Health and Wellness from New York University and completed a two-year post-graduate Advanced Trauma Studies program at the Institute of Contemporary Psychotherapy. She is trained in various modalities that inform a holistically based practice including EMDR, Internal Family Systems, Sensorimotor Psychotherapy, Energy Psychology, and Hypnosis. In 2012, she received the NYU Steinhardt Award for Outstanding Clinical Service.

Debbie speaks regularly to a wide variety of audiences, and is available to give presentations, workshops, and trainings.

To learn more about Debbie, please visit her website: *debbieaugenthaler.com* and join her Facebook community, *Grief to Gratitude.*